THE DYNAMIC LAWS
OF CREATIVE SELLING

TOM LEDING

God Bless you always
Thank you for being
Such a blessing
to us!

12/06

EP
EBED PRESS
NEW YORK

The Dynamic Laws of Creative Selling
ISBN 0-9741927-2-4

Published by Ebed Press
3125 Villa St.
New York, NY 10468
www.ebedpress.com

1. Money   2. Income   3. Motivational, Personal

Cover design by: Colin Smith
 www.pixeloverload.com

Printed in the United States of America

CONTENTS

The ability to sell creatively lies in you
How to turn creative ability into cash

To all salesmen everywhere:

I dedicate this book with fervent prayer and the hope that you will read it well; that you will endeavor to understand its principles; and that you will thus come to a vital realization of your creative power and ability. Your success will be my reward.

Tom Leding

Creativity has been built into each one of us
it's part of our design.[1]
Ted Engstrom

---

[1] Toler, Stan Dr., Minister's Little Instruction Book, (Honor Books, Tulsa, OK. 1994) page 26.

How This Book Can Help You

This is the true, and I think, gripping story of a young man's search for success in selling. As a youth, I dared to dream great dreams about the future in spite of a difficult early life. Eventually, I became one of the most successful individuals who has selected sales as a career, as a way to fulfill great dreams.

I only regret that it is impossible for me to visit you in your home or office and discuss with you, face to face, what I have written. In preparing this book, however, I have taken the reader into my complete confidence. Through the memory of my own early years in sales, I visualized myself in your shoes.

Many books on sales and selling end up being dull and uninteresting, making the reader weary instead of embued with new enthusiasm. As I wrote, I asked myself these questions many times:

- Is what I am writing interesting?
- Is it instructive?
- Is it inspiring?
- Is it putting forth the right ideas?
- Will it increase the reader's understanding?
- Will it contribute to his or her growth?
- Will it help the reader to become a better salesperson?
- Will it help the reader become a better person in life?

Every idea advanced in this book has one objective, and that is to interest you, to stimulate, instruct, and inspire you to fulfill your dreams.

Creative selling is both science and art. Science teaches you what to do, and the art of creative selling shows you how to do it.

Creative selling is the ability and art of increasing the satisfaction of the prospect. You do that by convincing the prospect that what you are selling will fulfill his needs and desires better than anything else like it.

Creative selling is an individual accomplishment that reflects your personal ability to create and the strength of your personality and way of thinking. Your particular qualities and attributes are unique to you. No one but you can develop them.

My purpose is to help you develop those attributes and talents by drawing on the latent abilities within you. During the past four decades, it has been my good fortune to talk to thousands of people in all types of businesses, in all walks of life, in all kinds of places, and under all conditions.

During those years, I sold both tangibles and intangibles through every conceivable selling method. I have been able to combine first-hand knowledge with experience. In the process, I have been able to make a first-hand study of the actions and reactions of people in all walks of life.

Through studying human behavior, I have gained insight into temperaments, dispositions, ambitions, aspirations, attitudes, likes and dislikes, and wants and desires. Combining this information, I have synthesized the most helpful points into this book.

Actually, this is more than a book. It is an entirely new plan of selling, setting forth proven methods for creating sales, earning a larger income, and enjoying greater peace of mind.

This is not the work of a theorist in an "ivory tower". It is the work of a stern realist, who has encountered all the problems and heartaches which you are encountering. It is the work of one who has solved many of the problems perplexing you in various situations at this very moment.

Years of experience, combined with reading, analyzing, and researching have given me proven abilities to influence people to buy and at the same time keep them as friends. It is impossible to describe in a short introduction all the ways this book can help you because every page has a message.

The information that follows and the powerful principles involved, if applied in your life, will give you a workable plan of creative selling. You will have a plan tailored to your abilities to bring results and enable you to sell anything.

Tom Leding
Tulsa, Oklahoma

CHAPTER 1

Sometimes
"Stubbing Your Toe" Helps!

One morning in 1968, I left my home in Tulsa, Oklahoma, and drove to my office on the way to visit a prospect. As I got out of my car, I suddenly felt a tap on the shoulder. Turning around, I saw a gentleman whom I had never seen before.

"Are you Tom Leding?" he asked.

When I replied yes, he inquired if I originally was from Arkansas.

"That's right!" I replied.

He shook hands, introducing himself as an attorney from Arkansas, which did not mean very much to me. Then he explained that he was an attorney for my uncle, Cecil Thompson of Clarksville, Arkansas, who had passed away. This man's law firm had been appointed executors of my uncle's estate.

The law firm had found I was one of the beneficiaries under my uncle's will. A sizable sum of money was waiting for me in Arkansas, the attorney said, and his firm was prepared to give me my inheritance at once if I went there.

He suggested that I accompany him back to Clarksville, which I did. Being too late in the day when we arrived, I made an appointment for the next day and found a place to stay for the night.

Next morning, I rose early. It was a beautiful spring morning with a clear sky and bright sunshine. The air was crisp, fresh-smelling, and fragrant with the odor of flowers and plants. It was a most invigorating day, and I was excited in anticipation of receiving my uncle's bequest.

In fact, I was walking on air, aglow with the hope and expectation of receiving a legacy that would allow me to fulfill my dreams.

Exactly at 9 a.m., I presented myself at the building housing a bank on the lower floor and offices above. The receptionist in the law firm's office was very gracious and most accommodating.

In a moment, the young attorney who had met me the day before came out of an inner office, greeted me cordially, and conducted me to the office of the senior partner.

The head of the firm seemed delighted to see me, the nephew of his old friend and colleague, the late Cecil Thompson. After I had showed him proof of my identity, he had me sign a few routine papers, which I was happy to do, still in great expectation.

At this point, the older man called his secretary and had her draw a check to my order.

Then he suggested that I might like to cash the check downstairs before returning home. I thought that was a great idea. Waiting until I got back to Oklahoma would mean a hold being put on the check until it cleared. Here I could get the money immediately.

The younger attorney took me downstairs to the bank, introduced me to a cashier, who would give me the money when I endorsed the check.

She asked me how I would like to have the money, and I said, "In thousand-dollar bills."

That did not seem to be a problem, as she walked over to the vault and casually returned with a hundred thousand-dollar bills, counting them out for me deliberately and carefully.

I placed the bills in an envelope and thanked both the cashier and, particularly, the attorney for his firm's splendid courtesy and expeditious carrying out of my uncle's wishes.

Placing the envelope very carefully in my inside coat pocket, I turned to leave the bank. Just as I reached the door, I "stubbed my toe" on something—and woke up!

How My $100,000 Dream Came True

At first, I was very disappointed and let down. The dream had been so vivid and undreamlike. However, as I pondered the dream, the thought came to me that I did not need to inherit $100,000.

All I needed was to "stub my toe," wake up, shake off lethargy, get out of the rut in which I was living, and come to a conscious, vital realization of the power of creative selling that I was sure was within me.

I began to firmly believe that development of this ability would enable me to make many hundred thousands of dollars.

However, I realized that in order to "claim my heritage" and derive the full benefit from creative selling, I would have to develop a definite and concrete plan of action.

At that time, I was attempting to sell life insurance without any orderly, scientific plan of action. I operated on a hit or miss proposition—mostly miss! Successful creative selling, like the inheritance from my uncle, was only a dream.

In that era, the typical general agent of a life insurance company was a sort of pompous gentleman. He would put his hands on your shoulders, rear back with an air of great authority, and hand you a rate book and some application blanks.

His words, "Now, go out into the world and sell," were the only training you would get as a salesman.

It was sink or swim on your own. So out into the world I had gone, and I had been floundering around like a fish out of water. I walked the streets, stood on street corners, and watched the people go by. Prospects, prospects everywhere, but not a single one for me. I had no definite plan of action as to how to contact any of them.

Now and then, someone would grant me an interview out of courtesy, but the inevitable reply was, "Sorry, not interested."

With sore feet, an aching back, a sour disposition, and both hands empty, I would wearily trudge back to the office.

This kind of day was repeated over and over.

I had begun to question, "What is the trouble? Is it me, or the company, or the life insurance business in general?"

After my dream, I decided to do something about this situation that seemingly was going nowhere.

How an Idea Gave Me Faith In Myself

First, I sat down and analyzed the principle of life insurance thoroughly to see if the problem was with the product. I concluded that, actually, life insurance is an excellent idea.

I liked the idea of the protection it can provide.

I liked the idea of the opportunities it can create.

I liked the idea of the savings account it can establish.

I liked the idea of the income it can guarantee for old age.

In fact, I liked the idea of all the benefits life insurance can provide for an individual and his or her family.

This scientific analysis of life insurance gave me a comprehensive interpretation of its function and a clear picture of its benefits. I became completely convinced that it was a good idea, a sound and practical proposition.

Next, I looked at the company. If there was a problem, it was in the fact that salesmen were not well briefed on the benefits of the product, nor were they trained at all in selling. However, the company and the agency seemed to be sound.

Therefore, the trouble had to lie with me:

If there was no training, I had to provide my own.

If there was no education in the life insurance field, I had to learn for myself.

In other words, my success in selling depended solely on me.

I had faith in my product, faith in the company, and I knew I could sell, so I had faith in myself. I had to develop a plan. To do that, I had to answer certain other questions:

- How could I convert this faith into results?
- How could I get across the idea of how beneficial life insurance could be to prospects?
- How could I convince a prospect that insurance was a

safe place to invest his capital?
• How could I make a prospect feel as I felt about life insurance?

Henry Bullis, former chairman of the board of General Mills, used to give his salespeople the following advice:[1]

> *"Forget about the sales you hope to make and concentrate on the service you want to render."*

> *"The moment people's attention is centered on service to others, they become more dynamic, more forceful, and harder to resist. How can you resist someone who is trying to help you solve a problem?"*

> *"The person who goes out to help [others] to a happier and easier way of life is exercising the highest type of salesmanship."*

---

[1] Bits & Pieces Magazine, (Fairfield, N.J.: The Economic Press), Vol. R/No. 29, pp. 10,11

CHAPTER 2

How I Converted Faith Into Results

It became apparent that the only scientific way to demonstrate my faith in life insurance would be to create a sales plan that would carry the message of its benefits and values to the prospect. I needed a plan that would convince a prospect of the satisfaction and peace of mind achievable through owning a policy or policies.

It was up to me to use my ability to sell by drawing on an inner strength of belief in the product and in myself to create a sale that did not exist before. "Head knowledge" and heart belief had to be translated into action.

To become a successful salesperson, you must begin where I did: Develop a right attitude toward yourself as well as toward your product.

You must realize beyond the shadow of a doubt that you are not merely "a rag, a bone, and a hank of hair." You are greater than the outward appearance of your body.

Your ability to think gives you the power to transcend the limitations of outward appearances. You can organize and visualize ideas and thoughts about your product strongly enough to communicate vividly to a prospect those same ideas and thoughts. True belief in, and excitement about, anything is contagious.

The organization of what you think and visualize about your product can be scientifically constructed into a definite plan.

What is a plan? A plan is a method or blueprint of action. It is a program of what needs to be accomplished, a design to carry a thought, a project, or a development.

Therefore, a plan is a concrete means to help you fulfill your desires, to create sales, and to render a useful service. Actually, to do this effectively, it is wise to have two plans: a plan of operation and a sales plan.

A plan of operation will govern, guide, and control your general activities. Organizing and arranging activities daily in order of priority will save time, conserve energy, and eliminate chaos. The orderly arrangement of time will guide and direct you through the labyrinth of the busiest day.

A sales plan will govern, guide, and direct your sales procedure. Prospects are influenced and motivated to action by ideas. The more quickly they receive ideas about the value of the product, the sooner they will act.

I concluded that life insurance guarantees many valuable benefits to a prospect and to his or her family. Therefore, I came to the conclusion that the quickest, the most practical, the most efficient, the most feasible, and the most scientific method of carrying that idea to the greatest number of prospects in the shortest period of time would be by means of such a sales plan.

Essentials of a Good Sales Plan

I had plenty of prospects once I had a plan for how to approach them, but no good sales approach. I saw that it would be only good sense on my part to create a sales plan that would set forth in plain, understandable language the many benefits and values of life insurance and what that meant to the prospect.

Such a sales plan had to be good, compelling, and solid. It had to contain the power to attract the attention of a prospect and the power to arouse a prospect's interest. It had to stimulate the desire of a prospect to own a policy.

Many hours of study and meditation were spent in creating this sales plan. I checked, double-checked, analyzed, and visualized all the aspects of sales that I could see.

Was my plan interesting?
Was my plan concise, yet comprehensive?
Was my plan stimulating?
Was my plan persuasive?
Was my plan convincing?

Every idea I had, every sentence, and every detail was studied with the strictest attention. I studied every word for the correct pronunciation, the correct enunciation, and for the right sound and inflection.

Every thought in each sentence was studied for proper emphasis. Every specific detail of my plan was weighed and balanced. I took nothing for granted and overlooked no detail knowingly.

When I had my plan in good form, I memorized it. I read it out loud many times. I dramatized it. I felt it, lived it, and perfected it. Then I used it.

My sales plan presented a good proposition based on a sound idea. However, I am sure you are wondering if it worked.

Were prospects attracted?
Were they interested?
Where they stimulated to act?
Were they convinced?

The fact is that the results of my sales plan exceeded my best expectations. That sales plan has sold millions of dollars worth of life insurance.

Learn a Lesson From Actors

In presenting a sales plan, it would pay to learn a lesson from actors. On the stage, on television, on the screen, and on radio, an actor or even an anchorperson on news shows has been thoroughly trained in a correct and precise way to deliver his or her lines or reports.

Actors seem to give every sentence, every word, and

every gesture its proper place and timing. Their deliveries look natural and spontaneous, but believe me, they are trained to do this right.

They feel and seem to live their roles right before your eyes, and you get caught up in their parts and live them right along with those delivering the lines.

Suppose, however, they came on stage or on the TV set not knowing their lines?

Suppose they know what they are going to say but not how to say it?

What do you think the sponsors of the programs or the producers of the films or plays would do? The actors or anchor people would be fired, and the networks or producers would be justified in so doing.

Performers know their lines because they want to attract and please "prospects"—you, the audience. By pleasing you, they please the sponsors, who please the networks or the makers of films and producers of plays.

If it pays to know your "lines," your sales pitch, in order to get paid well in the news and entertainment businesses, it certainly will pay you and me as salespersons.

If it pays even more to study and know how to deliver those lines, it is worth money in selling to do so as well.

This was the realization that caused me to create my sales plan and to perfect my delivery of it. The end result is that I was not performing or conning prospects, I believed every word that I said.

My faith in my product and in myself produced results.

I came to realize that a good sales plan was the means to achieve my end, which was a successful, financially rewarding career once I set out to put that plan into practice.

A Good Sales Plan Gets Results

A good sales plan enabled me to concentrate all my inner strength and focus all my abilities on arresting the attention of a prospect.

A good sales plan enabled me to kindle interest, stimulate desire for my product, and convince a prospect to move from hearing to believing as I did and then to doing.

A good sales plan enabled me to get results quickly and meant money in my pocket, as well as benefits for the prospect.

When I "stubbed my toe" in my dream, I woke up to the power of creative selling. That result has been worth many times more to me than the inheritance in the dream. It can be worth the same to you, provided you "stub your toe" and wake up to your potential.

If I can do it, so can you. The will to win is not as important as the will to prepare to win. A poem, whose author is unknown to me, makes the "bottom line" to this chapter:

> *He worked by day and toiled by night.*
> *He gave up play and some delight.*
> *Dry books he read, new things to learn,*
> *And forged ahead, success to earn.*
> *He plodded on with faith and pluck,*
> *And when he won, others called it luck!*

CHAPTER 3

Your Place in Our Economy

Selling is not a new art, but is as old as mankind. When men first began to exchange ideas, they began to engage in trade. They first bartered or "traded" something they owned for something someone else had. As the population of the world grew, a monetary system representing things or labor was developed.

Selling always has been used as a means of influencing someone to buy something you want them to buy.

Selling has been demonstrated in the form of exchanging ideas, products, plans, or services. Obviously, sellers learned quickly that, in order to influence someone, you had to please him or her.

Someone who is pleased will listen and pay attention to your story. Otherwise, that person is bored and will lose interest, very quickly ceasing to hear what you are saying. This development opened up an entirely new area of selling.

Those selling something, be it ideas or material things, learned that it is necessary to discover the personality characteristics of the one being approached. A successful salesperson must learn the prospect's wants, needs, hopes and aspirations, and other hidden factors that influence the desire to buy.

In addition, a salesperson is compelled to turn a "searchlight" on his or her own human nature and personality. Most importantly, a thorough knowledge of whatever is being sold becomes necessary. The history of the product, its components, its functions, and the benefit or value it will add to the life of the buyer must be understood.

In any age, the "market" had to be analyzed in order to comprehend the possibilities of a product. The salesperson had to learn to uncover needs known and unknown to prospects, how to supply those needs, and how to create markets for needs that might not have existed before.

Today, a salesperson is no longer an order-taker with a battered briefcase, a bag of tricks, a bundle of sales cliches, and a stock of stale stories.

A successful salesperson must be a psychologist, a scientist, a business analyst, a student of human nature, and an artist all rolled into one.

A professional salesperson deals first of all with the greatest attribute of mankind: the mind and ideas as applied to the continued development of a thriving economy and the distribution of products within that economy.

This development in the role of sales in the economy brought the need for creative selling.

The Need for Creative Selling

Creative selling has a very definite place in our economy. It is the only "driver" that can keep the economy strong, balanced, and capable of expanding to meet new conditions developing in today's shaky environment with lightning rapidity.

These new situations and conditions require new products and new services. Only the salesperson can create the new markets necessary for their success.

Men and women who sell are not only faced with a responsibility but, after 9/11, with major challenges. They must have the daring and ability to sell creatively. They must "stub their toes," wake up, and shake off lethargy.

Arouse the sleeping giant of creative power and positive action hidden within yourself. As a salesperson, you must dare to think for yourself, to rely on your own creative power.

With faith and confidence, you can draw on your latent abilities to practice and demonstrate the power of creative selling in ways that others may think impossible.

Those who blaze new trails, open up new markets, pioneer new products, and create sales are those who dare to sell things that have not been sold before. While others doubt, they go forward. They think, they seek, they ask, they search, and they find. They open new opportunities and help to furnish employment to millions of people.

They dare to take the challenge of unknown territory. They have the incentive to undertake and the urge to begin, and soon their abilities are turned into power that produces sales.

Creative selling is a science and also an art. The science teaches you what to do and the art shows you how to do it.

Creative selling is the art of increasing the satisfaction of a prospect by showing that person your product will best fulfill his or her needs and desires. That, in essence, creates a market that did not exist before.

However, the first obstacle to creative selling is negative thinking.

How To Overcome Negative Thinking

Creative selling is an individual accomplishment that embraces your personality and your strength of mind and will to enable you to "march to a different drummer." If your thinking runs along the "ruts" of a previously plowed field, you are limited by the thinking of those who came before you. Many times, this leads to negative thinking.

Of course, some of those who preceded you in your field did not "fall into ruts" but made their own paths. Creative selling takes ideas from those innovators and breaks new ground. However, no one but you can find and develop your qualities and attributes.

Cut yourself loose from negative thinking and petty restrictions of "this is the way it has always been done." Tradition will hamper your thinking. Examine past ways and methods. Then take the best from them and build new ways.

Negative thinking, "pygmy" ideas, and resistance to change are weights that hold you back. Open up the channel of positive thinking that will get you out of the negative "ruts" and let your own particular creative abilities empower you to success.

Cast aside doubts and uncertainties. They are of no value.

Turn the light of positive ideas and hope on doubts, worries, and dreads. There are no shadows where light prevails. Negative thoughts are of the darkness and cast shadows on what creativity you dare to put forth. Expect nothing but good results. Rejoice and be glad that you have the ability as well as the opportunity to sell.

You will find it a thrilling experience to serve those with whom you come in contact by meeting their needs. If you get rid of negativity, each morning will bring the excitement of starting anew. What seemed a burden and a task will become an interesting and profitable adventure.

In their latent abilities and creative power, men and women who sell will find they have undeveloped resources to help build and rebuild the economy of the nation. They are the keys to unlimited prosperity and to furnishing the good things of life to a greater number of people for many years to come.

New and better products are coming into the market every day and new wants and needs are being discovered nearly every day. Each person who sells or is preparing to sell has an unparalleled opportunity to partake of the good things of life and to share them with other people.

Opportunity is not just knocking on your door but is urgently ringing the doorbell!

Opportunity is an open door urging you to avail yourself of the greatest aggregation of untapped wealth and prosperity this nation or any other has ever known.

The potential of selling is greater today than ever before and greater are the possible rewards. However, courage is a major requisite for moving through the door of opportunity.

How Courage Gives You Authority

To move into creative selling, you have your own "row to hoe," your own life to live, your own sales pitch and procedures to follow. I hope some of the ideas in this book will help you to be courageous and put your own creativity into action. If so, you cannot fail to be successful.

Courage is a spark from Heaven.

Courage fills you with the faith to act, and faith gives you the strength and dynamic power to perform and move ahead. No one knows how good he or she is until courage is put into action.

Courage is that quality that enables you to encounter any situation with firmness.

Courage makes a person daring and bold, fills you with valor and the dauntless spirit to conquer all adversities, overcome all obstacles, surmount all conditions, solve all problems, and hurdle all hindrances.

Courage does not mean being without fear. It means moving ahead in spite of fears. Move out in courage, and creative power will be aroused within you. You will make sales you never thought possible.

Courage will enable you to increase your sales production a hundredfold and keep our economy prosperous and expanding as you learn how to make your efforts pay off.

How To Make Your Efforts Pay Off

Harness your abilities, discipline your efforts, measure your time, marshall your energies, and concentrate your selling abilities. Your efforts will be rewarded with success.

Submerge your own desires and needs in those of the prospects. Care about the prospect's needs more than you do your own. Make the prospect's interests your cause and do not worry about results. They will take care of themselves.

Be aware that courage and creativity have a subtle enemy, as dangerous as fear and doubt. That is procrastination. The old adage that procrastination is a thief of time is true. It also saps your energy and hinders your efforts.

Indecision and postponement bring many delays and rob you of many valuable sales. Take hold of yourself. Believe you can sell, and you will have the ability to sell. Courage has genius, power, and magic in it.

- Are you bold?
- Are you determined?
- Are you really serious about selling and in earnest about a sales career?

Once you begin to operate in creative selling, you will

have all the vim, vigor, vitality, forcefulness, and power you need. You will get results. Your success and progress will be fascinating and stimulating, and perhaps, beyond your own comprehension.

Learn to be bold and courageous, but at the same time, remain humble and not arrogant. Many people cover doubt and fear with pride as a mask, and prospects soon can tell the difference between real creativity and fake. Sooner or later, that person will "become a cropper."

Every ounce of real effort invested in selling will be justly rewarded and fully compensated.

The days ahead of us demand strong minds and understanding hearts, fortified with a will to succeed, enlivened by creative ability, based in true faith in ourselves and our nation, and acted upon by ready and willing hands.

An inscription found written in gold letters on one of the pillars of the main court in a Wanamaker department store in Philadelphia is this:

> *Let those who follow me build with the plumb of honor, the level of truth, and the square of integrity, education, courtesy, and mutuality.*

The admonition using builder's tools (the plumb, level, and square) as graphic images of life was written by one of the greatest salespersons in our history: John Wanamaker, founder of the department stores that carry his name.

Arnold Palmer, a well-known golfer, has the following plaque inscribed with an anonymous poem hanging on his wall:

> *If you think you are beaten, you are.*
> *If you think you dare not, you don't.*
> *If you like to win but think you can't, it is almost certain*
> *that you won't.*
> *Life's battles do not always go to the stronger woman or*
> *man, but sooner or later, those who win are those who think they*
> *can.*
> *Things work out best for those who make the best of the way*
> *things work out.*

CHAPTER 4

How To Attract the Prospect's Attention

Inspired by her Bible reading, a salesperson from Akron, Ohio, wrote a letter early one fall morning in 1940 to the famous minister and author, Dr. Lloyd C. Douglas.

In her letter, Hazel McCann wrote, "As I was reading in the book of John about the crucifixion and how the soldiers had cast lots for the seamless coat of Jesus, this was my thought, `What might have been the reaction of the Roman soldier who won the coat? Did he wear it? Is there any legend about that man?'"[1]

Just a week later, she received a reply from Dr. Douglas:

> *Almost every day, I hear from someone who thinks he or she has found a good idea for a story, but only once before have I had an idea handed to me which seemed to have large possibilities. It was very kind and thoughtful of you to give me the benefit of your luminous idea, and I shall try to do a story on it that will fulfill your expectations.*

As a result of Mrs. McCann's idea, Lloyd Douglas wrote a book that has sold more than two million copies, been translated into seventeen languages, and made into a classic film at the cost of $4 million dollars. That book and movie is entitled The Robe.[2]

Countless millions down through the centuries had read the Apostle John's account of the crucifixion of Jesus the Christ. They had read of the soldiers who gambled for the seamless coat He wore, but there is no record of any reader considering the reactions of the soldier who won.

Mrs. McCann was creative. She considered the situation and had an idea, but she did not stop there. She passed the idea along to someone with a track record of creative thinking. Dr. Douglas became her "prospect." She caught his interest, seized his attention, and stimulated his desire to write another book.

He was convinced that her idea was the seed of a wonderful story and was sold on that idea. Then he acted upon his decision. As a result, the late Lloyd Douglas is almost more remembered for that book than any other he wrote. Her idea benefitted not only the author, but the millions who have read or seen the resulting book or film.

The highway to the interest of any individual runs across the fertile plain of ideas. Mrs. McCann used that highway to attract Dr. Douglas' attention. As a result, she was highly rewarded even if not monetarily.

A salesperson has access to this highway from a choice field of selling ideas. A salesperson must be able to present an idea or ideas by creating a plan to merchandise a proposition.

You must turn over what you have in order to get something else. In short, you must sell your idea.

You must keep on the move and consider the ups and downs in your activities as stepping stones to great achievements.

Have you ever thought about why ocean waves constantly roll and break against each other with clocklike regularity? Without this persistent motion, the ocean would become stagnant. Everything in and around it would die. The movements of the waves keep the water teeming with life and vitality.

Ups and downs in selling act as a tonic to provoke thought and stimulate action. The world is a proving ground for ideas. The prospects on whom you call furnish material for your laboratory of human relations.

Your salesmanship is the "head chemist" compounding formulas. If those formulas are successfully compounded, you can attract the prospect and sell whatever you desire. In this chapter are formulas compounded in the laboratory of human relations, tested in the field of experience, and proved on the grounds of hard knocks.

How To Use the Law of Attraction To Make Sales

The laws of the universe are abstract until we begin to understand the principles involved. Then we discover that these laws are interactive in all areas of our lives. According to science, the universe is held together by "the Law of Attraction." Physics tells us that this law is a force that acts mutually between particles of matter, tending to draw them together.

A law of attraction also operates in the field of sales. This "force" is the formula, the process, the method, the plan, and the action you use to attract the prospect. The more you know about the prospect and the situations that control his actions, the quicker you can attract him.

Attracting the prospect calls for a combination of science and art, as I have mentioned before and will continue to stress. Science instructs us what to do, and art teaches us how to do it.

Through observation, experience, reflection, and reasoning, a salesperson can analyze a prospect. You can uncover the reasons that influence and motivate a prospect to act. Prospects are governed and motivated to action by ideas, as was Lloyd Douglas.

Compounding ideas into a scientific sales plan and presenting them in logical sequence stimulates reaction which leads to quick results. Human nature is fundamentally the same. You can be fairly certain what reaction you will get when you present prospects with a certain definite idea.

A positive idea in action always produces a reaction. This reaction will be favorable if the plan to convey the idea is scientifically prepared. An important key to this preparation begins with you. You must know yourself better than your prospect.

The Importance of Knowing Yourself

A knowledge of yourself and what appeals to you often gives you a clue as to what appeals to and will attract others. Most prospects are fundamentally alike, so you must discover an appeal that causes them to act. What will appeal to one usually will appeal to all.

Most of us are constantly trying to persuade and convince ourselves that we are different from everyone else. My forty years of experience in selling and experimenting in the laboratory of human relations has convinced me to the contrary.

We all have a lot in common. The sooner we realize this, the sooner we will be on the right track to attract prospects. We must appreciate one basic fact about a prospect: He or she has desires, problems, and needs, and usually will listen to a reasonable and commonsense appeal on how to meet and fulfill them.

Your first steps in creative selling should be to understand what the prospect thinks; and, based on this, set out to develop a specially tailored well-formulated sales plan. Using the prospect and his needs as a center of interest, you can build and create a sales plan that will impel the prospect to act. You can attract and inspire him to have full confidence in your proposition.

---

[1] Years ago, I read this anecdote about the origin of the idea for "The Robe," but at this point, I do not have the origin.

[2] Douglas, Lloyd C., "The Robe," (Boston: Houghton Mifflin, 1999, new ed.).

CHAPTER 5

Governing "Sets": Sources, Interests, Desired Advantages

In analyzing the average prospect, we find that decisions to buy are controlled by three important sets of threes: Sources, interests, and desired advantages.

The three sources that control sales ought to be integrated into your activities and appropriated for your use. They are:

1. The prospect has a desire which is an unfilled want.
2. The prospect has an urge that stimulates buying.
3. The prospect has a reason to buy based on one of the other two sources. He has definite knowledge of an established need.

After distinguishing the nature of the sources that control the prospect's buying, you then must uncover the situations that prompt the three sources, the first of which is interest.

Each individual has many interests. However, if you were able to sift through them, you would find only three main interests in life. On these three are based most of a prospect's reasons for buying.

1. The main interest usually is providing for family.

2. The secondary interest usually is his or her vocation or business.
3. Of third importance is fulfilling wants, comfort, and pleasure.

Obviously, I have listed those three in the priorities of most family men or women. Singles may put the third interest in first priority. Prospects who are workaholics might rank the second one first. Discovering the order of importance of these interests is an important part of knowing your prospect.

In analyzing the sources and interests that cause buying, we find these first two sets of threes can be influenced by whatever advantage the product is perceived as having on them. What advantage will your product give to his or her desires, urges, and reasons to buy and on the fulfillment of meeting family needs, business needs, and personal needs?:

1. Will the product bring happiness or peace of mind?
2. What advantage will this give his or her health?
3. What financial advantage will be obtained?

Again, you must study your prospect in order to see which of these three advantages has priority.

• Does the prospect derive happiness for himself or his family from what he buys?
• Do his purchases buoy up his spirit?
• Does he feel he is doing something really worthwhile?

Most prospects place a great value on health as the most important asset in life. He or she will buy almost anything if convinced the product will improve or safeguard personal health or that of family members.

Most prospects understand that it is necessary to spend money to make money. Therefore, when the product is one on which profits can be made by resales, this is a major reason to buy. This brings us to another basic element of the law of attraction: giving in order to receive.

You Must Give in Order To Get

This principle makes a direct road to the prospect's interests, a direct road to the source of the decision to buy, and a road map of the advantage by which he or she can be attracted. These roads all converge as the foundation on which a scientific sales presentation can be constructed.

With knowledge and information about the prospect that give you the sources controlling the decision to buy, the interests underlying the sources, and the advantages the product will bring, you can create thoughts and ideas to attract any prospect. By knowing these things, you can gain his or her confidence and then sell your particular product.

Ideas concerning your product built around the prospect's interests, needs and wants, and confidently conveyed by you, will convince that person to buy.

The law of attraction is very plainly expressed in the Bible:

> *For unto every one that hath shall be given, and he shall have abundance: but from him that hath not shall be taken away even that which he hath.*

> Matthew 25:29

As this principle is applied to attracting a prospect, it simply means that if you have the thoughts and ideas to do so and give them out, you also attract other things to you. More ideas and thoughts will be attracted to you.

On the other hand, if you do not make use of the thoughts and ideas you have, even those will disappear from your mind. The law of the universe that you have to give in order to get is inexorable and immutable.

In selling, you have only one thing to give: your ability, intelligently reviewed and appraised, conveyed to others through a system or plan of action. You create this sales plan in a reasoned, scientifically conceived way or in a haphazard, hit-or-miss way. To attract a prospect, it must be the first alternative.

The perfecting of your selling ability rests with you:

- How high in the scale of performance do you register?
- What are you doing to improve your efficiency?
- Have you learned how to harness all your abilities and concentrate them on the job of selling?
- Have you acquired the knowledge and skill to do the greatest amount of work with the least possible amount of effort in the shortest period of time? In the words of an old saying, do you use your head for something other than a place to hang your hat?
- Can you get maximum results with minimum effort?
- Can you adjust to different circumstances and adapt quickly?
- Can you apply common sense?
- Do you assume the role of self-importance when given the responsibility of serving others or do you fulfill your duties humbly?
- Does arrogance affect any expert knowledge you have so that your sales ability loses charm and effectiveness?

Remember that if the product or service you are selling could talk on its own and reveal its qualities, merits, usefulness, benefits, and advantages to the prospect, your services would no longer be required.

As a product cannot do this, it is your responsibility to present it effectively. This requires positive thinking, creative planning, and dynamic action.

The Ability to Sell Creatively Lies Within You

The power of creative selling lies not in the product, not in the service, and not in the prospect. Creative selling power lies in your ability to apply the law of attraction to draw the prospect to you.

As a salesperson, you want results. You want to make a sale, and you want to be of service to the prospect. The most scientific and practical way to do this is to give the prospect all the knowledge and information possible about your product.

Make an effort to give him or her a complete and comprehensive picture of what the product is, what it can do for the prospect, and the pleasure and satisfaction to be derived from owning it. You stimulate and incite his or her consciousness with a genuine reason to buy. Your persuasion causes the prospect to act.

The prospect says, "This is an appeal to my reason and to my interest. According to my judgment, it is a sound presentation. It makes sense. This salesperson is telling the truth and believes what is being said. Therefore, I am going to act on this advice and counsel."

You need to demonstrate that the product you are selling has merit in faithfully promising to meet the needs and wants of others. Your prospect sees that the product will therefore serve and benefit him or her.

How To Turn Creative Ability Into Cash

To gain attention and interest in your product is not enough. Through a feeling of confidence and earnestness, you must arouse the desire of the prospect for what you propose. You do have the ability to concentrate your thoughts. The sale will build itself if you center your thoughts on it.

Thoughts turn into realities when they cause you to act on them.

You can apply the law of attraction as a means to help you put the power of creative selling into action. It will turn your sales ability into cash. After all, this business of selling narrows down to one thing, just one thing: taking your product to the prospect.

Take the words of Walter LeMar Talbot as a motto, and you cannot help but succeed [1]:

> *Show me any man of ordinary ability, who will go out and earnestly tell his story to four or five people every day, and I will show you a man who just cannot help making good.*

[1] Bettger, Frank. How I Raised Myself From Failure to Success in Selling, (Englewood, N.J.: Prentice Hall Inc., 1949).

CHAPTER 6

How To Create a Sale

The most important secret of successful salesmanship is to find out what the other fellow wants, then help him find the best way to get it. Always talk about what the prospect wants.

Some years ago, I read about a man who hired an opera house in a small Pennsylvania town for one night but engaged no ushers or other staff. About a month before the date for which he had engaged the hall, he had a prominent billboard plastered with these words in huge letters: HE IS COMING!

A week before the scheduled evening, this sign was replaced by these words: HE WILL BE AT THE OPERA HOUSE THURSDAY NIGHT, OCTOBER 15, AT 8:30!

That evening, the man himself sat in the box office and sold tickets at $4 each to a capacity audience. When the lights went up and the curtain was pulled on the stage, all the crowd could see was another huge sign reading: HE IS GONE!

In spite of its being a fraud and scam, all the principles of successful selling are wrapped up in this story:

- Attention was gained.
- Interest was developed.
- Desire was stimulated.
- Prospects were convinced to act.
- The deal was closed when they bought tickets.

Obviously, I am not recommending this trick, because one very important item was missing: a "product" was not delivered. Therefore, there certainly would not have been any "repeat" sales.

However, the four basic elements that "sold" this scam are the same as those necessary for any sale. In this chapter, I want to unfold and develop these principles and learn how to apply them to create a sale or to improve your present sales plan.

When I was 12 years old (more than fifty years ago), I began to sell, and I am still selling. In fact, I get more real pleasure and enjoyment today out of selling than ever before. Selling gave me a modern "school" and a complete "laboratory" made up of living people. This afforded me the opportunity to study many phases of human behavior and to understand the relationships that exist in various aspects of sales.

Selling, in particular creative selling, is the greatest and most interesting study in the world to a true salesperson. There must be an idea before there can be a product or service. There must be an invisible thought before there comes a visible thing.

Therefore, if mankind has the capacity and ability to create a product or service by the means of an invisible idea, it stands to reason that we have the power to create sales and to establish a market for that product or service. This is the line of reasoning, the trend of thought, that I have always followed, and it has never failed.

I know from personal experience that a demand and a market can be created for anything, even a product that never existed before. However, there are steps in the creative process that must be followed.

A Good Sales Plan Can Create a Market

My sales experience includes products such as vacuum cleaners, paint, roofing, varnish, electrical appliances, shoes, books and directories. It includes services, such as advertising of all types and insurance of all kinds, especially life insurance. Due to circumstances, it has been necessary for me to create a market, a demand, for everything which I have sold.

My sales experiences not only involved creative selling but were backed by a strong incentive: Create a market or starve! Selling was never a question of my finding prospects, however. I always had more prospects than I could possibly visit. In order to cover the available prospects effectively and efficiently, necessity forced me to develop a good sales approach.

Therefore, I spent many hours creating and preparing a good, solid sales plan around the product or service I was endeavoring to sell.

This plan had to have qualities and attributes to attract the prospect's attention, engage his interest, and stimulate his desire. It also had to be dynamic enough to convince, motivate, and impel the prospect to action. My plan had to focus a prospect's attention on my proposition to the exclusion of all others.

Gain the Prospect's Interest by Your Interest in Him

In selling, I always try to remember that the prospect in his office or home has never seen or heard of me and, naturally, is not particularly interested in me.

The only way to engage a prospect's interest is to bring his or her attention to focus on me because I am interested in him or her and on my product as something that will add to happiness, health, or wealth. After all, there are only three main things involved in a sale: you, the product, and the prospect.

In geometry, we are taught that a straight line is the shortest distance between two points.

In selling, you will find that the distance between you and a prospect is a sale. A sales plan makes the straight line that shortens the distance.

Usually, it is easy to get an audience or interview with a prospect, but gaining that person as a customer with whom you do business requires creativity.

To achieve the objective, you must "hit the bull's eye," to use a shooting metaphor. Your "weapon" may be the best, but if you have no ammunition in it or if your aim is off, you are not going to hit the center of the target. The "bull's eye" in selling is the sale, and your bullet or ammunition is a prepared sales plan aimed at the center of the target, your prospect.

A creative sales plan uses the right bullet, not one with too much or too little powder. It is absolutely impossible for you to give the prospect all the knowledge and information that you possess about your product. That would be like birdshot that scatters over the target but does not hit dead center.

Telling about your product in too much unnecessary detail merely confuses prospects instead of giving them a clear picture of what you are trying to do for them. Instead of making a sale, you possibly will encounter an ignominious defeat. That is known as "overkill." On the other hand, a weak sales plan is like using a BB gun to try and bring down a deer.

You need to take the best, most pertinent, facts about your product and shape them into your creative sales plan. This will avoid giving the prospect information in a haphazard, hit-or-miss way, but in an orderly, scientific plan designed for the size of the quarry, so to speak.

Before entering the life insurance field, I had prepared and used successfully many different sales plans to sell many different products.

I wondered how in the world I could sell a life insurance proposition with only a rate book to show prospects. To me, the rate book was the key to a large "safe deposit box" containing millions of dollars in cash assets. How could I convey this idea to a prospect?

Basically, I was convinced people would listen to me about life insurance because I felt I could gain the attention of prospects. My confidence at that point was based on experience. I had been successful in gaining the attention of prospects about many other products and, after all, these were the same prospects who would need life insurance.

To use another metaphor as a picture of selling, I began by planting some "seeds."

You Must Plant Ideas To Harvest Sales

Selling is no different than farming. In fact, selling is a great deal like farming. Before gaining a harvest, the farmer must plant seed. He knows he must sow before he can reap. A farmer plants seeds; a salesperson plants ideas.

Your ideas, like seeds, will never grow a crop unless they are planted. You reap, like the farmer, according to what you sow. The more ideas a salesperson plants, the bigger his harvest, the more sales he will reap. In order to reap a harvest of life-insurance sales, I knew I must "sow a crop" of life-insurance ideas.

The seeds, I realized, must be condensed information concerning the real value of life insurance and the advantage it would mean to a prospect and his or her family.

The seeds must contain the possibility of growing to a harvest of peace of mind for the prospect. The idea of purchasing a policy must satisfy his or her sense of caution, need for security, and feeling of safety for family members.

Therefore, I needed to create a sales plan around the needs of the prospect, convincing him or her in a nutshell that life insurance would satisfy those needs. In creating and developing this sales plan, I studied my product from every angle, not overlooking a single phase.

I sought every available source of knowledge for information to create my "seed".

I read every book I could find on the subject.

I compared the products of each major life insurance company.

I analyzed all types of coverage: term insurance, ordinary insurance, 20-payment life insurance, all kinds of endowment life insurance, all forms of annuities, and all forms of retirement-income plans.

I reckoned with mortality tables, compound interest tables, life expectancy tables, cash reserves, disability clauses, and tables and clauses concerning optional settlements.

I studied the protection life insurance affords partnerships, executives of corporations, and individual proprietors.

I researched tax laws relating to wills and trusts. I familiarized myself with inheritance tax laws, both state and federal. In addition, I carefully weighed, analyzed, and considered the social, economic, and financial aspects of life insurance.

As a result of all my research, I found that the institution of life insurance was one of the sustaining pillars of the American economy and worthy of the attention of any prospect. After becoming thoroughly saturated with information relating to life insurance, I began to study the prospect.

Where was the prospect's place in the great network of economic, social, and financial relationships? How would all this knowledge interest and benefit a prospect?

I found the entire system of life insurance was set up for one purpose only: to serve the needs of prospects. I found a life insurance policy is a declaration of financial independence. Such a policy embodies guarantees that solve the prospect's worries about family finances after his or her demise, solve his problems, and even answer retirement questions.

A life insurance policy will help the prospect to realize hopes, ambitions, and dreams as well as satisfy needs. However, a prospect would not be aware of all the wonderful things life insurance could do for him. It was up to me, the salesperson with the knowledge, to get the pertinent information to the prospect.

In creating a sales plan for life insurance, I found that I had a lot in common with prospects. Each of us has a family, home, job or career, and in all probability, a lot of unfulfilled desires.

A verse by a man named Douglas Malloch graphically tells of the common humanity between most of us.[1]

> *There may be nothing wrong with you, the way you live, the work you do. But I can very plainly see exactly what is wrong with me.*

> *It isn't that I'm indolent or dodging duty by intent. I work as hard as anyone, and yet I get so little done. The morning goes, the noon is here, before I know it, the night is near, and all around me, I regret, are things I haven't finished yet!*

> *If I could just get organized! I oftentimes have realized that not all that matters is the man; the man must also have a plan.*

With you, there may be nothing wrong, but here's my trouble right along. I do the things that don't amount to much of any account, that really seems important though, and let a lot of matters go.

I nibble this, I nibble that, but never finish what I'm at. I work as hard as anyone, and yet, I get so little done. I'd do so much you'd be surprised, if I could just get organized.

---

[1] Bettger.

CHAPTER 7

Organizing and Presenting Your Sales Plan

It is very simple to build a sales plan, and it begins with reversing Malloch's complaint in the poem at the end of the previous chapter: just get organized.

Building a sales plan is no different in concept than building a house. A mass of material thrown together will not build a house. Every brick, every plank, and every nail must be put in the proper place. The same is true of a sales plan.

A sales plan is organized information, which sets forth the reasons why the prospect should buy your product. The most scientific way to create a sales plan is to get all your material together. Get all the facts you can about your product, just as I did about life insurance.

Investigate its history, background, relationship to the economy, and the part it plays in life. Analyze the data. Catalogue the facts, organize them, define them, and then refine them. After that, take the ones that fit best into your prospect's life and needs.

Include in the "blueprint" anything that will improve the prospect's business, increase his or her wealth, and add to the welfare of the prospect. Feature anything that will contribute to the prospect's peace of mind or enrich his or her happiness.

Organize your sales plan in sequence, have each step ready to enumerate point by point, and speak in concrete terms, not abstracts or generalities. Make your plan brief, concise, direct, definite, forceful, and above all, understandable. Season it with the savor of personal interest, flavor it with the spices of enthusiasm, and sweeten it with kindness.

Learn to appreciate one major fact about the prospect: he or she is a rational human being with problems and needs who is ready to listen to a suggestion on how to meet them based on reason and common sense. By thinking this way and seeing prospects as "real" people whom I could help, I was able to fit a life insurance policy around each prospect's shoulders like a cape.

I made the sales plan reveal the benefits of my product and what they could mean to the prospect and his or her family. You can do the same for your product and your prospects. Once you have a creative sales plan, you must study the best way to present it.

The Importance of the Right Presentation

In my sales plan, I refer to the prospect as "Mr. Doe" or "Ms. Doe" and to the insurance company as "Everyman's Life Insurance Company."

When I call on a prospect, I say in a friendly and positive manner, "Mr. (Mrs. or Miss) Doe, my name is Tom Leding," being careful to pronounce my name very distinctly.

Then I say, "'Everyman's Life Insurance Company' is offering a combination life insurance and investment plan to business and professional people. This plan does four definite things for you."

Then I enumerate the four things:

"This plan immediately creates an estate for you and your family. Unlike most estates, this plan never depreciates in value and is always worth a hundred cents on the dollar. It is free from all liens, mortgages, and liabilities and can be administered for your family so as to be exempt from certain taxation.

"This plan establishes a savings account for you after the

second year. A very valuable feature of this savings account is that it is always available. It is ready at a moment's notice to furnish you with ready cash to cover any unforeseen contingencies or emergencies.

"This plan pays all future deposits for you in the event you should become totally disabled through any kind of disease or accident. This guarantees that your estate and your savings remain intact.

"This plan makes it possible for you to retire with an income for life at any age between fifty and sixty-five. This income will be guaranteed to you as long as you live. You have absolute assurance that every dollar invested in this plan will be returned either to you or to your beneficiaries."

The above creative sales presentation contains about two hundred words and only requires one and a half minutes to deliver. It does not attempt to tell the prospect everything you know about life insurance in technical terms. However, it does present the benefits in a true and concise statement of facts.

It presents a comprehensive overview in an understandable way of what life insurance will do for the prospect and his or her family. The presentation is spoken in a language any prospect can understand immediately.

In most instances, the prospect sees this is an opportunity to do something real and practical for his family and for himself. He will be adding to his family's welfare and to his own happiness and peace of mind.

A prospect probably will think, "An estate for the family, a savings account for an emergency, a retirement income for me. What more could I want?"

The word "estate" is dynamic. It conveys the impression of wealth and affluence. The very word gives the prospect a sense of importance, adds to his sense of dignity, and buoys his self-respect. An "estate" conveys a plantation in Louisiana...an oil field in Texas...a ranch in California...an orange grove in Florida — or it may mean a life insurance policy.

As you can see, choosing the right words in which to present your plan is extremely important. The prospect does not want to hear what you know about something. He wants to hear what your product will do for him.

The Right Word in the Right Place

To be effective, words spoken in the "language" of the prospect are subtle and indestructible forces that convey the impression that the idea is his or her own. The right words penetrate the mind, persuade the prospect of the truth of your facts, and convince him or her to buy your product.

Every word in your sales plan should be studied, weighed, and analyzed from every standpoint.

Does each word convey the meaning intended by you?

Will that word give the prospect the right idea?

By analyzing and considering words in this fashion, you can select the right word for the right time and place. Words in your sales plan that convey the value of the product are the impelling and motivating forces that create a sale.

Spoken in a cheerful and optimistic tone, the right words make it easy for a prospect to say yes. It is surprising how much little things count in selling. Words and smiles may seem like small things, but they carry tremendous weight.

There is an old saying to the effect that boulders can be seen by anyone, but pebbles will cause you to stumble. Little things such as using the right word in the right place, cultivating a friendly attitude, a pleasant voice, and agreeable disposition, and a high regard for the prospect are "pebbles" that, if taken into account, will make a sales approach much smoother and easier.

I always approach prospects in a genuine spirit of humility, because I believe I can help them. My attitude is that of one who has come to serve them. As long as I present my sales plan humbly but confidently, it has power and punch and gets results.

It is good to be wise, but not to give the idea that you are smarter than the prospect. Give him or her credit for being as smart and wise as you, the salesperson, are. In today's world, it does not pay to try and bluff your way through a presentation. Most prospects can tell brass from gold any day.

Answer any objections honestly in the form of suggestions. Let the prospect run things in your interview. Remember: He who treads softly goes far.

Behind words are thoughts, which must be strong and

forceful in sales. However, to win and influence prospects, words must be clear, concise, and agreeable.

How To Put Power Behind Thoughts

Ideas developed into clear thoughts must then be expressed in words. How those words are delivered puts power behind your thoughts. To use the building analogy again, ideas are the blueprints, thoughts the materials, and words the tools that complete the sales.

Thoughts cannot remain indefinite abstractions, if you are to be successful. They must be vital, living forces that reveal the merits of your product, its qualities, its value, and what it means to your prospect.

Words are the last, important element in any sales pitch, conversation, confrontation, dialogue, or discussion. However, words without forceful, creative thoughts will lack power and punch.

Forceful thoughts transmitted in the right words give your sales approach color, form, essence, substance, power, and dynamic force. They clarify and define the way you present the product with simplicity. They give the product meaning in your mind which you then can express with conviction to the prospect.

This creative sales plan makes the prospect feel about the product as you feel, even if he or she does not know all the details and information that you do. A scientifically prepared sales plan will increase your knowledge, give you a more comprehensive understanding of your product, and revolutionize your sales procedure.

Forceful thoughts expressed in confident words will give you more courage and a keener zest to go after more business. This creative sales plan, which you develop for yourself from knowledge of the product, will increase and improve your ability to attract prospects. It will rekindle your enthusiasm, if you have gotten into a rut of routine thinking.

One of the pitfalls people over forty can fall into is thinking it is too late in life to change careers or to succeed in an old one. The simple fact is that it is rarely too late for anything!

There have been many examples of people succeeding even at the normal retirement age.

I know of one man who was more than sixty years old when he turned down an offer of $200,000 for a successful restaurant only to have the state bypass his location with a new highway. The result was that his business went down the drain leaving him with only a social security check on which to live.

Most people would have been crushed by such a blow, but this man refused to give up. Instead, he took stock of his resources and realized there was one subject about which he was an expert—how to fry chicken. I am sure you can guess who this man was.

He kissed his wife goodby, climbed into an old, battered car with a pressure cooker, a can of specially prepared flour for batter, and set out to sell his recipe to other restaurants. At first, it was tough going, and he slept in his car many nights for lack of enough money for a motel room.

However, a few years later, the late Col. Harlan Sanders of Kentucky had built an enormously successful fast-food chain called Kentucky Fried Chicken, now franchised worldwide.

The famous opera diva Beverly Sills once said: You may be disappointed if you fail, but you are doomed if you don't try.

Price Pritchett of Pritchett & Associates, consultants on organizational change, wrote in one of his books:[1]

> *Frankly, the world doesn't care about our opinions. Or our feelings. The world rewards only those of us who catch on to what's happening, who invest our energy in finding and seizing the opportunities brought about by change.*
>
> *And change always comes bearing gifts.*

---

[1]Pritchett, Price. The Employee Handbook of New Work Habits for a Radically Changing World, (Dallas: Pritchett & Associates, Inc., 1994), paragraph from the Introduction.

CHAPTER 8

Why the Prospect Buys

Common sense tells us that the only reason a prospect buys is because he would rather have the thing he buys than the money he must pay for it.

A salesperson must make a comprehensive survey of his industry and a careful analysis of the product. He must have all the answers or as many answers as he possibly can. A creative sales plan must answer questions in advance to cause the prospect to want the product more than the money he will pay for it.

More than two centuries ago, a tall, powerfully built young man took up residence in Philadelphia in a second-floor room of a lodging house at Seventh and Market streets. Every day and late into most nights he worked over papers on his desk developing a "creative sales plan." Many days, two consultants visited him to help with this plan.

These men had a tremendous job on their hands. They had to develop a plan that would sell an idea of tremendous importance to many prospects, all at one time.

Their task was to convince the delegates of the thirteen American colonies to the Continental Congress that independence from the mother country was not only desirable but possible. They had to "sell" the Declaration of Independence to prospects who had many questions about the "product."

That young man was wise, prudent, and knowledgeable. He had a great vision which he was incorporating into a sales plan to give the delegates a new idea translated into new thoughts. This idea, which he shared with a handful of others, involved a new slant, a new conception, and a new meaning of government. Then the delegates would return home to "sell" their constituents on a new reason for becoming independent.

July 4, 1776, this plan was presented to the delegates, and its power, force, and impact have been felt down through history. Even today, the reverberations are still being heard around the world. The men who took the idea of liberty for all and transformed its accompanying thoughts into a concrete plan, of course, were Thomas Jefferson, Benjamin Franklin, and John Adams.

In my opinion and that of many others, the one great idea that sold independence from England is found in the second paragraph of that great sales plan:

> *We hold these truths to be self-evident, that all men are created equal, that they are endowed by their Creator with certain inalienable rights, that among these are life, liberty, and the pursuit of happiness. That, to secure these rights, governments are instituted among men deriving their just powers from the consent of the governed.*

In those two complex sentences, Thomas Jefferson scientifically, skillfully, and concisely set forth the bottom-line reason why the "prospects" should buy the plan. The delegates understood the idea, the vision, behind the words, the thoughts and reasons for "buying" Jefferson's creative plan, and were convinced to act.

Thomas Jefferson, in spite of being a Deist who did not believe in the supernatural sections of the Bible, gave us a succinct explanation of God's principles of government on earth. Those two sentences sum up the biblical plan for man to govern his fellowman.

Jefferson gave us a great lesson on how to apply the principles of creative selling and how to give power to a sales plan. He reasoned out in advance what the delegates desired, what the new country which they represented needed, and answered in advance as many of their questions as possible.

In accepting his plan, the delegates were convinced they and their families would enjoy a new freedom, a more complete security, and as a result, greater peace of mind and prosperity. The "product" was worth more to them than the "currency" of the struggle to "buy" freedom.

Like Jefferson, in developing your sales plan, it is only wise to anticipate any questions a prospect may have.

Anticipate the Prospect's Questions

In order to anticipate the prospect's questions, ask yourself these questions:

- Where does the product fit into the prospect's life?
- How can the prospect make use of the product?
- What need of the prospect will the product satisfy?
- What main reason will convince the prospect to own it?

After all, people take action in any area because they have been persuaded to do so, by self or by someone else. In selling, you want to know the specific reason that will persuade your prospect to buy.

There can be many reasons why a prospect buys a product. However, the main reason a prospect is "sold" is because the salesperson is able to put his or her finger on a particular reason for a particular prospect at a particular time. You have a particular reason for buying something, and so does a prospect.

A prospect does not buy a tube of toothpaste for the same reason that he or she buys a ton of coal. Neither is a house purchased for the same reason as a life insurance policy. The purchase is made according to the satisfaction of needs or desires expected to be derived from owning the product.

Understanding this principle enables you to know the particular appeal to make in order to cause your prospect to act. Knowing that conserves the prospect's time and increases your sales efficiency.

"Homing in" on the right motive for buying makes it unnecessary to spend half an hour talking before a prospect discovers what you are trying to do for him or her.

When you discover the particular reason your particular prospect has to buy, then you can tailor your sales plan around a product based on that reason. Basically, there are five reasons people buy.

Five scientific reasons a prospect buys

I will list the five reasons, then give an illustration for each one. Finally, I will create a sales plan built around that reason, a plan that will demonstrate the efficacy of knowing your sales approach. The five major reasons are:

1. Need of the product
2. Usefulness of the product
3. Adds to the prospect's wealth
4. Satisfies pride
5. Satisfies caution (need for security and protection)

We talked about this first reason—need of a product—in an earlier chapter. A lot of things fall into this category, such as food, clothing, and shelter. However, a prospect must make choices from many, many products that fit his or her personality or particular situation.

Need of the product

For an illustration, let us look at a "biggie," buying a house. Here are a few suggestions to incorporate into a sales plan in order to find and satisfy a particular prospect's need:

Start with a description of a possible house. Cause your prospect to visualize large, spacious, comfortable rooms with lots of fresh air and sunshine set in beautiful grounds. Picture a beautiful tile bathroom with a spacious tub and a kitchen and pantry that will make cooking easy and a joy. Point out that the dining room overlooks the terrace.

On the other hand, if the prospect leans toward smaller, more convenient homes, show an open plan that can be divided into several living areas. Show how compact and useful this design can be. Perhaps a condo or town home will better fit this prospect's needs? Then stress the lack of maintenance and the security of the building.

Describe the neighborhood next, unless your prospect is more concerned first of all with where this residence is to be, then reverse the order of needs. Does the prospect favor friendly neighbors and schools nearby for children? Then find one like that. Does the prospect "need" something close to shops or out in the country? Find out, then make your sales plan fit that.

Thirdly, discuss transportation facilities. Is the house easily available to police and fire departments? Is it on the bus line, if the prospect does not own a vehicle? Are the roads easily navigable, kept in good shape, and close to interstates? Incorporate all the factors into your sales plan that will meet the prospect's needs. Obviously, first find out his or her particular needs!

Discuss the construction of whatever structure you have chosen to meet his needs. Point out the quality of the workmanship, the quality of the materials, and the attention that has been paid to details and added amenities.

Lastly, deal with maintenance costs. Explain assessment values, interest rates, and taxes. Hopefully, all those will be low enough to meet the prospect's needs so that he or she can enjoy the residence without being financially stressed.

Usefulness of the product

Buying things for their usefulness adds to the prospect's enjoyment, health, and happiness, as well as to the well-being of his or her family. These things include television sets, radios, pianos, household appliances, vehicles, even books and videos. For an illustration, let us pick a television set.

Does your prospect watch TV for sports, news and documentaries, dramas and mysteries, or for cultural programs? Knowing that, you can tailor your sales plan to fit the best set at the lowest price. Where is the set is to be placed? A huge set in a small room would be overpowering and hard on the eyes while too small a screen in a large room defeats the purpose.

Your plan must convince him or her that the cost will be worth it for the hours of relaxation, enjoyment, and expanded knowledge. Point out, if there is a family, that watching TV together can enhance family togetherness. Also, a function to stress is the ability to oversee what the children will watch.

Incidentally, if the TV set is a cabinet one, check out the decor of the prospect's home and point out the kind of finish and material to complement that. Some prospects desire the latest high-tech developments, which means a salesperson must be familiar with the latest and newest in television technology.

The same set of suggestions is true of someone buying an automobile. A prospect buys a vehicle for its usefulness in business, for its usefulness to the family, or for his own enjoyment, comfort, and happiness. A salesperson must first find out the reason for which a vehicle is being sought and the price the prospect is willing to pay.

Possible ideas to deal with in this sales plan are the economy of operation, the life of the tires, the safety rating of this vehicle, plus the reputation of the firm making the product. A salesperson might speak to the prospect along these lines:

"Mr. Prospect, this car is large and roomy with lots of baggage space. The seats move into position with the touch of a button and add to your comfort while driving. You and your family can look forward to many enjoyable weekends and vacation trips."

Or, "Mr. Prospect, the brakes on this vehicle are the last word in precision and safety. You can stop almost instantly, which means added protection for you and your family on the highway amid "hot rods" and other drivers who are careless."

Adds to the prospect's wealth

A prospect whose motive for buying falls into this category bases purchases on whether or not they add to his wealth and/or possessions which reflect wealth. In building a sales plan to sell stocks, bonds, or other financial assets, even life insurance, you want to center the prospect's mind on five important advantages involved in investments. It will help to organize these advantages by priorities:

The safety of his financial investment: Provide the prospect with the name of the corporation backing the investment. Relate to him its assets, liabilities, and surplus. Tell its history, showing financial standing, operations, average earnings, and progress for the past 10 years.

Guaranteed income: For example, in the company's 10-year history, it has never missed giving dividends and never failed to honor its coupons. With this record, it is fair to assume its future income will be assured.

Tax exemptions: If there are any, explain these.

Potential increase in value: Project the trend of this product to increase in value based on favorable circumstances in the economy.

Marketability: Prove that these securities are listed on the stock exchange and can be converted into cash at a moment's notice.

A sales plan built around these five advantages will put additional securities in the prospect's strongbox and commission checks in your bank account.

Satisfaction of pride

This type of prospect buys to satisfy his personal wants, to impress others, and to satisfy pride in his or her looks, appearance, or position in society. Suppose you are trying to sell this person a suit of clothes.

Try the following sales plan: Make an appeal to the prospect's dignity, but do it with tact and diplomacy.

Some prospects will declare that they cannot be flattered, but will fall for a compliment on the fact that they cannot be flattered! Show the prospect that he or she will "look like a million dollars" in this suit.

Direct attention to the cut of the suit, the quality of the fabric and the wide range of colors available.

Display the expert workmanship and point out that expert tailoring guarantees a garment whose perfection will be obvious to anyone who sees it on the prospect.

Guarantee delivery at any time the prospect wishes, giving the feeling that this suit has been made exclusively for him or her. This is a personal touch anyone would like and impresses the prospect with your interest in his welfare along with a sale.

A sales plan incorporating these ideas will impel and stimulate a prospect to buy, putting a suit in his or her wardrobe, and a check in your pocket.

Satisfying Caution

The prospect in this category wants to be assured of personal security and that of any family members. He or she wants to make sure that personal needs and wants will be provided for, as well as family needs. Perhaps old age is looming up, a time when most of us would like to be financially independent.

Purchases for this prospect must contribute to peace of mind and add to the welfare, happiness, and comfort of self and family. Security is why most prospects buy life insurance.

In creative selling, you should not talk as much about the product as about what it will do for the prospect. Your product is simply a means by which you want to bring about the thing of underlying interest to the prospect. You want to keep reminding the prospect that your product will add something to his life.

In the creative presentation for life insurance used as an example earlier, notice that I never use the word "I" to the prospect, only "you" and "your." In the initial presentation, I focus on his or her needs and motives for buying.

I present the product in basic, general terms. Initially, nothing is said about the various types of insurance, the laws of probability, or mortality tables. No mention is made of cash reserves or any other technicalities.

Again, it is not necessary that a prospect know everything the salesperson knows about a product, only about what it can do for him or her.

<u>How To use these reasons</u>
<u>To make sales</u>

To this point, I have discussed the psychological attributes of prospects and have listed five reasons why someone will buy a product. These reasons apply to all prospects, no matter what race, sex, social class, or field of employment.

With a simple change of definitions, any number of products can be sold with the creative sales plan I have described. Your ability to sell your product lies in you. You can build a sales plan that will arouse a prospect's imagination, attract a hidden desire or want, and move him or her to action.

A good way to begin your day is with a reminder to yourself, an affirmation of your abilities, something like this one of mine:

> *This is the beginning of a new day. God has given me this day to use as I will. I can waste it or use it for good.*

> *What I do today is important, because I am exchanging a day of my life for it. When tomorrow comes, this day will be gone forever, leaving in its place something I have traded for it. I want that thing to be gain, not loss; good, not evil; success, not failure, in order that I will not regret the "price" I paid for it.*

CHAPTER 9

How To Turn Objections Into Sales

Before the Korean War, I sold paint, cement roofing, and allied products in Oklahoma and Arkansas. The prospects on whom I called had never heard of the particular line I was selling. It was necessary for me to create my own market, and of course, I encountered a variety of objections.

When is someone a prospect?

Someone becomes a prospect when he or she will listen to your presentation. They must listen before they can offer a reasonable objection. One thing you must understand, however, is that the minute the prospect offers an objection, he or she is interested.

An objection does not mean a lack of interest.

The prospect sincerely has a question which you need to answer, or he or she is challenging the salesperson's ability or knowledge. In reality, the prospect is giving you a definite clue as to how to proceed.

In the latter case, what is really being said is, "Okay, I'm listening, but I am still from Missouri. You will have to show me."

Many objections are based on inner prejudices. When they are, the prospects are judging or sizing up your proposition prematurely. In these instances, prospects are failing to give due consideration to your plan.

You might say, he or she is not really listening, but filtering what you are saying through preconceived wrongful ideas.

The prospect is being unfair to you and to himself. Perhaps some earlier salesperson turned him off, turned out to be a "con man," or in some way misled him or her. Now all that prejudice and resentment is being taken out on you.

Another reason for objections is an excuse to postpone considering the product or the need it will meet.

In addition to valid-question objections, reactionary objections, and excuse-objections, there are other kinds of objections. The point for the salesperson is to not allow the prospect the slightest opportunity to doubt or distrust you.

Never tell him anything you cannot prove and back up factually. As a working motto, in place of the proverb *caveat emptor* (Let the buyer beware), substitute *caveat vendor* (Let the seller beware), and you will keep your balance.

I have sold many different products and services to many different people over more than four decades. In that time, I have encountered objections frequently and been able to turn them into sales. The principle on which I operate is to make full use of my ability to think and my capacity to act.

The application of thought can turn a reasonable objection into a sale, can turn a prejudice into favor, can deal with any other kind of objection fairly. The trick is to discipline yourself beforehand to think before calling on a prospect, to think while you are in the presence of the prospect, and to think after you leave the prospect.

You can change your product, your sales technique, even your prospects. However, you can never change human nature. By knowing your product and knowing all you can about prospects, you can adjust to human nature.

I could fill a book with nothing but experiences I have had in dealing with various kinds of objections. Following are a few typical examples, how I dealt with the objections, and the results obtained.

How To prove an objection is groundless

Once while selling in Arkansas, a very large concern in a small town was on my calling list. This firm supplied surrounding territories with roofing and paint products. The proprietor was sitting on the front steps shaving a pine board with a large pocket knife, a hobby known in the South as "whittling."

He greeted me cordially, and I presented the facts about the cement roofing I was selling in a sales plan I thought was very illuminating and most convincing. He listened intently, hardly batting an eye until I mentioned that my roofing was absolutely fireproof.

He burst out vehemently, "I don't believe a gosh darn word you say," and he took a sample jar of the cement roofing from my case, removed the lid, and stuck the long blade of his knife into the thick fluid.

He lifted the blade with its load of fluid over his head, then smeared it over the pine board on which he had been whittling. At that point, he pulled a book of matches out of his pocket, struck one, and applied it to the roofing. Instantly, it burst into a conflagration!

During his entire demonstration, I had remained calm, cool, and collected, because I had done my homework. Instead of heading him off and explaining why he was wrong, in spite of the demonstration, I wanted him to complete his experiment and see for himself.

After he declared triumphantly, "There is your darn cement roofing going up in flames," I calmly said, "What burned was benzine added to the asbestos compound of which the roofing is made to preserve it in a liquid state so it can be easily applied.

"When the cement is spread on a roof, the air instantly evaporates the benzine. What is left is roofing cement in one solid piece that is holeproof, nailproof, windproof, waterproof, fireproof, and foolproof."

I reached in my sample case, produced a board coated with the roofing product and from which the air had evaporated any benzine. I invited the prospect to set this board on fire. Without hesitation, he tried. Because I had done my homework thoroughly, I was able to have full confidence in the outcome. He was unable to do so.

He discovered I had told him the truth, so he sold himself. I let him answer his own objection, and his doubts and uncertainties evaporated like the benzine. He ordered three carloads of cement roofing at that time.

Don't Sell the Product, Sell Its Advantages

In 1955, I was engaged as a salesman to help put a new brand of toothpaste on the market. Soon, I found that the major objection I ran into was its newness. Prospects did not know about its advantages. Therefore, instead of selling the product, I sold the possibility of increased sales and good will.

In visiting a drug store, for example, I would say, "Mr. Pharmacist, I have an unusual plan that will make a lot of new friends for your store. This plan is hidden in the secret formula of a new and unusual dentifrice.

"This toothpaste cleans and polishes the teeth, preserves the enamel, eliminates tooth decay, cools and purifies the breath, and leaves a clean, wholesome, and pleasant taste in the mouth. Whenever your customer uses this toothpaste, he is going to think kindly of you, and when he needs other toilet articles, he is going to think first of your store."

This sales plan worked, and in one day in Tulsa, Oklahoma, I opened up thirty-four new accounts for this previously unknown dentifrice. According to records, it was one of the greatest feats in American salesmanship up to that time. The sales plan worked because I had anticipated the main objections and answered them before they were asked.

Time went by, and I found myself selling lubricating oils and again faced with objections. This time it was because the price was "too high." Of course, I knew already that my product cost more than some others commonly used.

My answer was like this: "A less expensive product costs you twice the price of mine, because you have complaints and mishaps that lose customers for you.

"Into my product go quality materials and excellent processes that add up to a top-notch performance. My product eliminates friction, increases efficiency, and lengthens the life of any machine. Its high grade performance is the result of years of experience and specialized know-how.

"My company —an old hand at this game as you know— produces this lubricant at the least possible cost and sells it at a fair price. If a less expensive method produced the same product, we would be the first to use it and lower the price."

An objection to price was overcome by proven quality and performance.

Did my presentation work? I soon sold three times as much lubricating oil as any other salesman in my organization.

How Creative Thinking Deals With Objections

At last, I found myself selling what is considered the toughest thing in the world to sell: a piece of paper with a promise to pay, a life insurance policy.

Life insurance is an intangible product that requires the highest form of creative selling. It used to be said that anyone who could sell life insurance could sell anything, even ice cubes to Eskimos or safety razors at a barber's convention.

In this field, I encountered thousands of objections. The ones that follow will give you some food for thought.

One day, I called on a prospect, and after I presented my sales plan with all the skill I had at that time, he suggested that I send him a "sample" policy. However, I had learned from hard experience how to deal with this objection.

I said, "First, let me tell you a true story about another man who liked to put things off. Many agents called on him from time to time, and he always suggested they send him a sample policy. The other day, he passed away, and after his death, his wife went to their safe deposit box thinking her husband had made ample provision for her and their children.

"She found ten sample policies for $10,000 each–$100,000 worth of sample policies that were not worth a penny. I was one of the guilty parties who had called on him. Now, I am sure I was not fair to his wife and children. I should have put more effort into persuading him to buy a policy rather than aiding and abetting him in procrastinating.

"In this case, postponing action not only was a thief of time but of the well-being of the man's family. Do you think I would be playing fair with your wife and family to send you a sample policy? I feel that would be a betrayal of them, and I want you to know that, right now, I represent them in this matter. I owe them a debt of responsibility."

This got under Mr. Put-Off's skin and turned him into Mr. Buy-Now, who purchased a $125,000 policy. Objections often can be turned into reasons to buy.

A few days later, I called on a certified public accountant losing no time in giving him the full content of my sales plan. CPAs, of course, are very clever at figures, especially when they are using figures as objections.

He responded, "I can make more money by investing it myself than a life insurance company can make for me. I have $25,000 invested in 4 percent bonds that are yielding me $1,000 a year."

I said, "That is fine, but how would you like to double the value of those bonds immediately."

He quickly retorted, "You bet I would. How can that be done?"

"Very easily," I replied. "Simply invest them each year in a $50,000 life insurance policy. In so doing, you immediately double the value of your bonds from an estate standpoint. Instead of your family having a $25,000 estate, they will immediately have a $50,000 estate."

"Say," he exclaimed, "I never thought of that!"

So I sold "Mr. Correct-all" a $50,000 life insurance policy by taking his objection, putting a little thought to it, and handing him the answer as a suggestion.

Another example is a man I call "Mr. Won't-Buy," who owned a chain of drug stores. When I finished my sales presentation, he promptly let me know that he did not believe in life insurance and would not give ten cents on the dollar for all the life insurance in the world.

After a pause, I said, "Mr. Won't-Buy, this plan does not cost you ten cents on the dollar. As a matter of fact, this plan requires only about two cents on the dollar a year."

"Do you mean to say that you can get me a life insurance policy for an outlay of only two cents on the dollar each year?"

I replied, "That is exactly what I mean. If you make a deposit of $1,000, my company will deliver a policy to you for $50,000."

His objection was countered, and he was sold. There are other ways of getting around objections.

Constructive Suggestions Outweigh Objections

Once, I called on a very prosperous wool merchant after his very efficient secretary put me through a third degree as to my name, pedigree, history, and business qualifications. Then she wanted to know what my purpose was in wanting to talk to Mr. No-Interest.

I explained my mission, and she let me see her boss. He listened very attentively, but when I finished my presentation, he very decisively said: "I am not interested."

Believing that discretion is the better part of valor and that a soft word turns away wrath, I said very gently, "Mr. No-Interest, I have never had the pleasure of meeting you before, but I ask you to do me a favor. Give me the date of your birth."

He answered that he did not give his date of birth to strangers. Whereupon I asked him to "loan" me his date of birth for a few days. He laughed, and the wall against life insurance got a crack in it.

In a few days, I returned and submitted a brief for his consideration based on his date of birth. He liked it, and as a result of circumventing his objection of "no interest," I sold him a $200,000 policy at an annual premium of $7,000.

Another man was not interested because he already had a very substantial estate. In the meantime, I had asked about his physical condition and suggested that I have a physician call and check him over. This he agreed to do.

Then I said, "You may have a large estate, but you could use $100,000 of life insurance to meet inheritance taxes, state taxes, and other administrative costs that will be imposed and assessed against your present estate. This fund will furnish the ready cash to pay expenses and leave your estate intact. In brief, why not let us underwrite the settlement costs of your estate?"

This suggestion cut through his objections, because he saw the wisdom of my plan. He bought the $100,000 policy.

Another call was on an investment broker, whose objection to life insurance was that he liked to speculate with his money.

I answered, "That is exactly why I called on you. 'Everyman's Insurance Company' wants to speculate with you. They want to wager $50,000 against your $1,200 that a year from today you will still be living."

He could not resist this wager, and his objection was "deep-sixed." He bought the $50,000 policy. You can see from these examples that the best way to answer objections is with facts or with constructive suggestions.

Another call I made was to a partner in a contracting firm, whom I call "Mr. Fish." His objection was that he was absolutely not interested. I remarked that I knew he was interested in his partnership, and I wanted to make a suggestion concerning it. He agreed to listen.

So I gave him a complete picture of a partnership and how it worked, which he already knew. However, he had not thought about my point, which was that the two most important things in his partnership were his life and that of his partner. I reminded him of the legal aspects if he or his partner passed away.

The death of either would automatically terminate the partnership and might wreck the business they had spent years building. I asked how much they had invested in the business, and when he told me, I suggested that the wise and practical thing to do would be for each partner to cover his interest by taking out a life insurance policy in that amount.

Then they should enter into an agreement that the proceeds from the deceased partner's policy would be used by the survivor, as beneficiary, to buy the deceased's interest out. This would make it possible for the survivor to continue in business without legal interruption or entanglement in the deceased's estate.

Mr. Fish said, "That is just what we want," and $200,000 of life insurance was placed on him and on his partner as a result of his "objection" and my suggestion as to how to get around it.

Again, I called on a prominent 54-year-old physician, who thought he was too old to profitably buy life insurance. I suggested that he invest some of his money in a $100,000 annuity plan to mature in eleven years.

He asked how that would work, and I explained, "In eleven years, if you are still living, you will get $100,000 in cash, or you can turn that money into an income for life giving you (at that time) about $19,000 a year as income.

"If you do pass away before you reach 65, your beneficiaries will get the $100,000 or the company could arrange for them to get a fixed, definite income as long as they live."

I left the doctor's office with a check to cover the first annual premium.

These experiences are not theories about selling. They are real-life illustrations of sound selling techniques. They are creative ways of getting around objections and will increase your sales as they did mine.

Creative Selling Can Increase Your Income

In reading these sales performances and the objections which they met, you should notice one important thing: My suggestions were simple, ordinary, practical ways of answering the prospects' questions. My technique was to present my ideas about the product in what I think of as a scientific sales plan.

I made suggestions honestly and straight from the shoulder.

I never exaggerated or faked the possibilities of my product.

I never used high-flown language or subterfuge as bombastic camouflage for my ignorance or for wrong motives.

I never made a claim or a statement that I could not back up with facts, but spoke sincerely and truthfully.

I never gave the prospect an argument but let him have his own opinion. Then I took his "buts" and handed them back to him in the form of suggestions that changed his thinking. His objections gave me information about answers which became sales.

When you apply the power of creative selling, you can concentrate, which produces quick thinking. Many constructive thoughts and suggestions will come to your mind, as you begin to think along positive lines in confidence. Your power to express those thoughts and suggestions will increase with experience.

In the end, your ability to do your job well while at the same time being of service to others will give you much satisfaction and many checks in your bank account.

Jimmy Reader has written that "our human potential is far greater than most of us ever dare to dream." He thinks we limit ourselves by small dreams. His "3-D formula for successful living" can be adapted to successful selling:[1]

- Dream big.
- Dare to be more than you thought you ever could be.
- Do all you can with what you have where you are now.

---

[1] Reader, Jimmy. Breaking Through to Your Highest Potential, (Tulsa: Honor Books, 1988, back liner).

CHAPTER 10

How To Perfect
Your Sales Plan

Man's first instructors were his eyes. He opened his eyes and was delighted with the things he saw. Then he discovered he had not only an eye to see the world around him but also a brain to interpret what he saw.

He noted, first of all, the many changes in nature. Through this observation, he discovered a law of nature that teaches a valuable lesson in selling. That is the law of repetition. As the law of activity is continually and regularly producing action in nature, the law of repetition continually and regularly repeats these changes.

Every day in the same way, the sun rises in the east and sets in the west with absolute precision. Night follows day with immutable certainty. The four seasons consecutively repeat their cycle with inexorable accuracy.

Repetition, educators say, is still the best way to learn anything. Almost everything you know was learned by repetition. As a baby, it took time to learn how to walk, but you kept repeating the same motion every day. Through experience (repetition), you acquired sufficient knowledge and practice to walk confidently. Once a difficult task, walking became automatic.

You learned to talk by the same law. As time went on and you began school, the same law manifested through human teachers who drilled you in the abc's, the multiplication table, and that first poem you recited before the class. The things learned by repetition are embedded into your subconscious mind as part of you. They became regular habits applied naturally and easily.

Repetition Makes a Sales Plan Part of You

The formation of habits—and not all habits are bad—has been likened to the making of a path across a field. After the first hiker has trodden down the grass, the next person is likely to follow the same path, and so on, until the grass is worn away. Everyone else walking that way will follow the same beaten path.

Constant repetition of something forms it into a habit. The law of repetition teaches you to perfect your sales plan and sales techniques. To put this law into action, practice your sales plan until you know every word of it by rote. Time your talk and repeat it until you sense the proper pitch and inflection to give each word.

The more you actually present the sales plan to prospects, the more confidence you will gain in it. You will begin to "feel" your lines and be able to give a reserved or an affable presentation as the situation requires. The sales plan has become part of you.

You will find the law of repetition has magic, not only for you but for the prospect. Through practice and demonstration, your sales plan gathers its own momentum. Your thoughts become magnets and you are able to discern the reactions of your prospect and sometimes the thinking that lay behind them.

The late great pianist and composer Ignace Jan Paderewski once said, "If I miss practicing the piano one day, I know it. If I miss for two days, my manager knows it. If I miss a week, my audience knows it!"

Continuous repetition produces perfection. Broadway performers still schedule two or more rehearsals each week, even after a run of years in a hit production.

76

It is said a certain pastor visited his church every day to preach. When asked why he preached six days to himself and only one to the church, he said, "It takes six days to convince myself, and only one day to convince my congregation."

One of the most difficult tasks in selling is to convince ourselves. Once that is accomplished, it is fairly easy to convince others, because sales presentations will be made with conviction.

The Importance of Conviction

Haphazard conclusions are the result of faulty reasoning. After thinking a proposition through, you can reach only one conclusion—it is true or it is false. If it is true, make a decision with conviction and act upon it with determination.

To realize the full impetus of ability and to derive its full benefit, a thorough and wholehearted conviction must permeate and embrace every phase of your occupation.

Knowing your sales plan thoroughly and your lines perfectly gives the added force of conviction. You have a greater urge to sell your product. Conviction engenders a spirit of enthusiasm, that inward intensity of being. Enthusiasm is that inspirational, vitalizing, propelling force you inject into selling.

You make whatever you are selling come to life through your dynamic authority when your sales plan rings with sincerity. If you can genuinely be enthusiastic about your product, it infuses in you an unfaltering trust and unbounded faith in it. The influence of enthusiasm is instantaneous, and the prospect is invariably inspired and persuaded to do business with you.

The Key to More Sales

The prospect never judges you by what you do not say. He judges you and your product by what you do say. If you can speak well, he or she will pay you. Your sales plan may be "old stuff" to you, but it is always "new stuff" to a prospect. Enthusiasm that builds conviction is like a master key to unlock many doors and usher you into many profitable sales situations.

I have given my sales plan on life insurance thousands of times, and I get as much fun and pleasure out of doing it today as I did years ago. My plan is as effective in selling life insurance today as it was years ago when I first used it. I believe and feel every word of my presentation.

Repetition has built a firm faith and unfaltering trust that sustains and stimulates me with fresh interest, new energy, keen zest, and unfailing confidence. Only by mastering your work will you learn to love it.

Some think memorizing a sales plan causes you to get bored and deliver your talk in a mechanical way. In my long experience of selling with excellent results, I have found just the opposite.

Practicing your sales talk until you believe it wholeheartedly and have enthusiasm and confidence, makes all the difference between few sales and many sales. By "honing" your skills in delivering your plan, you exhibit appreciation of the prospect's time and intelligence.

You know what you are going to say and how you are going to say it. You will not mumble, ramble, or stumble over words and concepts. You will speak with command. Instead of making you mechanical, repetition makes you positive and vital. It gives you self-confidence and an air of assurance.

Instead of feeling uncertain of your reception thus sounding shy and hesitating, repetition will cause you to sound and feel dynamic, bold, and courageous. Your sales approach becomes a living force and loses its routine, mechanical aspect.

Late great actors such as John Gielgud, Richard Burton, and Maurice Evans made the characters they played come alive. Yet on the stage, they repeated the same performance over and over, sometimes twice a day.

Did repetition make their performances mechanical? No, instead repetition gave life to their parts. Their lines were not only memorized but repeated until they became a vital part of the actors.

Perfecting Your Sales Plan Pays Off

Your sales plan is your "act." It is your means of serving a greater number of prospects. It is your meat and bread. When you perfect your sales plan, you can accomplish twice as much with less effort. This will give you more time to do the other things you like to do.

Therefore, it will pay you to use every effort to perfect your sales plan. Read it over, analyze it, meditate on it, visualize it, say it out loud, practice it, believe it, feel it, live it, demonstrate it, and note the effect that it has on the prospect. You will end up being surprised at your own performance.

In perfecting the sales plan, you are improving your ability to think and to use persuasion. This improves the power and accuracy of your claims. The one thing that will make your presentation mechanical is becoming discouraged.

It is a rare person who does not get discouraged. The answer to discouragement is one word: perseverance.

The value of courage, persistence, and perseverance has rarely been illustrated more convincingly than in the life of Abraham Lincoln. This is a much-told story, but well-worth repeating again.[1]

- Failed in business at age 22
- Defeated for the state legislature: age 23
- Again failed in business: age 24
- Elected to legislature: age 25
- Sweetheart died, according to legend: age 26
- Had a nervous breakdown: age 27
- Defeated for Speaker of the House: age 29
- Defeated for Elector: age 31
- Defeated for U.S. House of Representatives: age 34
- Elected to U.S. House: age 37
- Defeated for U.S. House: age 39
- Defeated for U.S. Senate: age 46
- Defeated for U.S. vice president: age 47
- Defeated again for U.S. Senate: age 49
- Elected President of the United States: age 51

Yogi Berra, renowned New York Yankees catcher who played in 14 World Series must have learned a lesson from President Lincoln and others like him, because one of Berra's famous sayings is, "Losing's a great motivator."[2]

If you have had a "losing streak" or think you can't win,

take a lesson from the many people who have lost and lost and lost before they won big. People who win have faith.

---

[1] Tan, Paul Lee, ThD., Encyclopedia of 7700 Illustrations, (Rockville, MD: Assurance Publishers, 1988), p. 1373, #6141.
[2] Guideposts, (Carmel, N.Y.: Copyright 2001 by Guideposts, Vol. 56, #12), p. 13 [Feb. 2002].

CHAPTER 11

The Power of Faith in Selling

Someone once asked the late famous financier and philanthropist Andrew Carnegie what he considered the greatest factor in his phenomenal success.

He answered, "Faith: faith in myself, faith in others, and faith in my business."[1]

Through that faith, Carnegie began his economic life making $3 a week and ended up giving away $3 million in his last 18 years.

Faith can be a religious belief or a system of religious beliefs (churches and denominations). However, another definition is "anything believed" or "unquestioning belief that does not require proof or evidence."[2]

So you see, faith is simply believing something or believing in something without proof or evidence. It means knowing something beyond the shadow of a doubt whether or not you can see it.

The world always makes way for the man who knows what he is doing and where he is going. I believe in myself. I believe in the prospect, and I firmly believe in my product.

I use only one yardstick of measurement in selling: If it is good enough for me to buy, it is good enough for me to sell. By applying this principle, success has crowned my efforts always, for which I am thankful.

Again, what is faith? Faith is believing in something. It is a firm belief or trust in a person, a thing, a doctrine, or a statement. It is a belief in the favorable outcome of anything undertaken.

The writer of the biblical book of Hebrews gave us the greatest definition of faith possible. He was referring to faith in God. However, the same statement is true of faith in anything: Now faith is being sure of what we hope for and certain of what we do not see[3] (Heb. 11:1).

The apostles had faith in the power of God and knew that the substance of all things was in Him and therefore invisible. They knew the evidence of that power was only a manifestation, or the visible thing.

Everyone cannot be a Henry Ford who invented a method of transportation that revolutionized the world from what was at the time the largest factory in the world covering seventy acres. His billion-dollar corporation has provided a livelihood for thousands, in addition to the advantages his invention gave to all of us.

Everyone in the United States, however, enjoys the same opportunities that Henry Ford, Andrew Carnegie, and others like them had. That is the "inalienable" right to "life, liberty, and the pursuit of happiness." Faith in oneself, next to faith in God, is the bottom-line foundation on which to pursue happiness, which includes succeeding in life.

With faith in the product and faith in one's self, every salesperson can double his or her present production and have a grand time doing it. In this chapter, I am going to give you a few hints and suggestions on how you can develop faith and apply it to your sales activities.

Two Kinds of Faith

The only possible way to get the correct answer to a mathematical problem is to conform to the laws of mathematics, based on truth. When you place your faith in them, you will always get the correct answer: two plus two equals four at any time, any place, or under any circumstances. Therefore your faith is based on truth that has been proven millions of times.

The second kind of faith has not been fully proven by experiment. An experiment may prove that it is true or may reveal that it is false. If experiment will prove the belief true, then it can be moved over into the first category. However, if the belief is false, then it becomes negative faith, faith in something that is not true.

Negative faith can be anything from those who believed for hundreds of years that the earth was flat to those who believe they cannot be a success! If you believe there is no way you can make it in life, then you are investing all your thought energy in negative faith!

Columbus' discovery of the "new world" while looking for a passage to India in 1492 opened the door for the understanding that the earth was round. Today, with proof, we laugh at those who, from the fifth and sixth centuries, believed the earth was flat because the Bible spoke symbolically of the four directions as the "four corners" of the world (Isa. 11:12).

By setting out to discover the perimeters of your own business world, in faith that you truly are going somewhere, you can laugh at the early part of your life when you believed your world was "flat."

Turn your faith from negative to positive, and you will find your belief was true.

How To Discuss Truth

Both true and false faith may be based on knowledge or information. However, false faith is based on erroneous knowledge and false or deceptive information. Those living in the Dark Ages built their faith on the false knowledge that if you kept sailing far enough you would drop off the edge of the world.

Therefore, I would modify that old saying, "Knowledge is power," to "True knowledge is power." False knowledge may be a tremendous burden, a serious impediment, a decided hindrance, and a very present handicap to your development and progress. Certainly, for years, the false knowledge that the world was flat hindered exploration and discovery.

Truth, in my humble opinion, means "an established law or principle with no exceptions." How is truth established?

Truth is discovered through experience and proven by experiments that test that law or principle over and over —and turn out the same way.

By experimenting with things you think are true, you can prove to your own satisfaction whether or not those things you believe really have a solid foundation. The man who discovered the components of water believed it was made up of hydrogen and oxygen and set out to prove it.

His experiments proved his hypothesis over and over, the same each time, giving us the chemical formula for water: H_2O. This became an established principle with no exceptions, therefore, a truth. Faith and belief turned into knowledge.

All things are governed by the immutable and unchangeable laws of God. The chemical composition of water reflects a law of God governing the physical makeup of the world. In fact, God is truth. Why do I say that? I assert that because truth is an established principle with no exceptions, and God never changes but is always the same (Heb. 13:8).

The late great scientist Albert Einstein reportedly once said, "The most incomprehensible thing about the universe is that it is comprehensible".

This is only another way of saying that everything comes within the range of our minds. The problem is that although thought is infinite, we do not discover truths until a thought on something is proven true. In other words, in another Bible law: faith without works is dead (James 2:20).

That does not mean salvation to a Christian is based on good works. It means that your faith is not worth anything unless you put it to work. Faith in God means living as much as possible as did Jesus. Faith in yourself means doing all things within your ability in the confidence that you can.

Just because man discovered the chemical formula for water does not mean that is when the formula originated. It had been the formula since the world began; man just did not know it.

Just because Columbus proved the earth was round in 1492 does not mean that is when it became round. The earth since creation has been round.

All the laws of physics, mathematics, and chemistry

always have been and always will be truths. All are established principles and truths. Mankind just did not know about them, so could not act on them.

The pyramids could have been lighted with electricity so far as the truth was concerned. However, no one knew until Benjamin Franklin how to begin to harness electricity.

The Egyptians building the pyramids did not know how to cut the lines of force, set up a magnetic field, and construct a dynamo to convert electrical energy into electrical power. An airplane could have flown over Bethlehem on the night of Jesus' birth, as far as the principle of aerodynamics is concerned. However, no one up to that point had even had faith in the principle enough to believe it, much less prove it.

Man does not create power; he merely discovers it.

We have been discussing principles and power in the field of material things, of the physical world. Yet there is a power greater than physical, and that is spiritual.

The power that sells is your faith in yourself based on the true knowledge of your product and your abilities. However, there is a Higher Power who can give your faith a boost and enlightenment to your knowledge of yourself.

Spiritual power operates best through the humble person. Perhaps you think all this believing-in-oneself leads to pride. Actually, a true knowledge of one's self and one's abilities should lead to humility. This old saying puts it best:

> *True humility is not to think lowly of oneself, but to think rightly, truthfully of oneself.*[4]

[1] Encyclopedia of 7700 Illustrations, p. 1000, #4345.
[2] New World Dictionary, Second College Edition, (New York: Simon & Schuster, a Division of Gulf and Western Corp., 1980), p. 2.
[3] The Holy Bible, New International Version, (Grand Rapids: Zondervan Bible Publishers, 1981, Copyright 1978 by New York International Bible Society), p. 916.
[4] Encyclopedia of 7700 Illustrations, p. 572, #2215.

CHAPTER 12

The Scientific Time and Way To Call on a Prospect

Time is a very important requisite in selling, and it is wise to conserve it. In order to do this scientifically, it is necessary to make a study of the habits of your prospects. Most prospects have fixed routines. Each day they go through approximately the same routine with certain hours to do certain things.

Through observation and study of people's habits and schedules over a period of almost half a century, I have discovered the best time to call on prospects. These findings will save you many hours of time, many sore disappointments, and perhaps many a sour disposition!

My findings will enhance your success greatly, for they will give you more hours to devote to actual selling which will increase your sales volume many times.

In calling on a prospect, it is advantageous to make lists according to the following three categories:

1. Those who are self-employed, business executives, and purchasing agents
2. Those who engage in professions
3. Those who are employed by others

Arrange the prospects on cards according to the category

in which they belong. As I have written earlier, it also pays to take stock of each prospect's temperament.

Temperament is usually revealed in his or her proneness to certain feelings, moods, or desires. These depend largely upon certain events taking place in his or her activities. These inclinations usually control the prospect's disposition for the moment.

A study of the prospect's inclinations in conjunction with his or her activities will enable you to approach the prospect at the psychological moment. This moment is more important in approaching a prospect than in closing a sale. The "scientific" moment to approach is aligned with the psychological moment.

At that moment, a prospect will be in the right frame of mind and in the right attitude to listen to your presentation. Over the years, I have studied the correlation between psychological moment and activities according to categories of work.

Self-employed, businessmen, and purchasing agents

In calling on executives, heads of businesses, and purchasing agents, I found the best time of day is after 10 a.m. Usually these prospects have a lot of routine work to do before this time: letters to dictate, orders to execute, authority to delegate, and plans to make for the day.

After that, the prospects usually are more relaxed. His or her focus has changed from "must-do" work to the next level of daily activities. The prospect's attitude has changed, leaving him or her in a better frame of mind to listen to your story. An approach at this time will merit consideration.

The next best time to call on prospects in this category is between 2 and 5 p.m.

Professional prospects

Physicians and surgeons have hospital rounds and outside calls to make, classes to teach, and meetings to attend. In spite of a heavy schedule, there are splendid times to call on them. These are between 9 a.m. and noon and 1 to 4 p.m. Another good time to call on those who live in the suburbs is between 7 and 9 p.m.

These "visiting hours" also hold true for osteopathic physicians, physiotherapists, chiropractors, and chiropodists.

Most dentists get to their offices rather early, but usually do not have appointments until about 9:30 a.m. The best time to call on them is between 8:30 and 9:30 a.m. By calling on a dentist before he begins dealing with his appointments, he is more disposed to listen to a sales approach. In all probability, an approach at this time will bring favorable results.

The time to call on attorneys is between ll a.m. and 2 p.m., working around lunch hours, or between 4 and 5 p.m. In between these hours, there are court dockets, seeing clients in office, or catching up with paperwork.

Stockbrokers, bankers, investment bankers, bond salesmen, and others engaged in the securities business can be called on to advantage before the Stock Exchange opens at 10 a.m. or after the Exchange closes around 3 p.m.

Contractors, builders, and others employed in the construction business can be called on before 9 a.m., at noon, or about 5 p.m. A large part of the day, these prospects will not be in their offices. However, to approach them, the hours mentioned are the best.

Professors or teachers will not be happy at being approached during school hours. The most practical time to call on prospects in this category is during the "letdown" period of the day, usually between 6 and 7 p.m.

Certified public accountants may be contacted almost anytime during the day. However, a good time of the year NOT to approach them is between January 15 and April 15. This is the busiest season for them, as they are preparing tax returns and finishing year-end accounting.

One CPA told me they are compelled to work day and night in March in order to eat in August!

Pharmacists and grocers usually have a slack period from 1 to 3 p.m. This makes a window of time for you to present your plan.

Insurance brokers and agents are in their offices from 9 to 10 a.m., generally also at noon, and again at 4:30 p.m. During this time, such professionals are approachable.

Those employed by others

Prospects in the publishing business should be called after 3 p.m. After a day filled with a lot of routine details, these men and women are ready for coffee and to relax a while by 3 p.m. That is the time they are open to listening to you.

Merchants, department store managers, and heads of departments can be approached anytime from 10 a.m. to noon or from 2 to 5 p.m.

Chemists and engineers are more available between 4 and 5 p.m. The best time to call on the clergy is anytime after Tuesday. Sundays are their busiest days, and Monday usually is their "rest" day.

Salaried people who earn less than $25,000 annually, along with all other wage earners, should be called on at home. These people include bookkeepers, secretaries and other administrative office workers, technicians, and government workers. The best time to call on these prospects is after dinner in the evening, say between 8 and 9 p.m.

Homemakers or housekeepers are best approached between 9:30 and 11 a.m. and between 1:30 to 4:30 p.m. If you ring the doorbell of a housewife before she has completed her morning chores, you are likely to get no answer at all or have the door slammed in your face.

The best time to call on prospects not covered in these categories will have to be ascertained from a study of their habits and inclinations.

No matter what time of day or year you call on any prospect, it is imperative to make a good first impression. Otherwise, you may not even get "a foot in the door."

How To Make a Good First Impression

Most prospects automatically are "on guard" when any salesperson appears, so it is to your advantage to prepare for this first hurdle in advance. A prospect begins an interview the same way you do, but from the other side of the door, in that he or she begins by sizing you up.

You have only two alternatives: to make a favorable or an unfavorable impression. It is rare to find someone who is so detached that you make no impression. By paying strict attention to certain predispositions, and by recognizing and respecting these, you can be assured of a cordial reception.

By ignoring your own "sizing up" of the prospect and just jumping foot first into your story, you may subject yourself to rejection or even derision. Certainly, you will lose even the opportunity to make a sale.

There is not only a "right time" to call on a prospect but a scientific way in which to approach him or her. In preparing your card file on prospects, enter each name according to its particular category. Copy the name exactly as it appears in the phone or business directory. Prospects, also like you, are very sensitive about their names.

A personal name is a symbol, a trademark, a badge so to speak, that distinguishes a person from the millions of other people in the United States. In most cases, a prospect likes his name or at least identifies with it. Usually the prospect likes to hear his name spoken and likes to see it in print.

When you first get your new telephone directory, do you look up your name to not only see it in print but to check the accuracy with which it was printed? If it is right, you may grin from ear to ear, or at least smile. A prospect is like that. In calling him or her, you must have not only respect but a high regard for the name by which each is called.

"What's in a Name?" Plenty!

A name is a perfect symbol. One letter in the wrong place or pronounced wrongly makes it imperfect. Therefore, when you call on the prospect, do not call him or her by the wrong name. That tells the prospect you are sloppy or that you did not care enough to get the name right.

The prospect will get the impression that if you are careless about something so important, you may be careless about other things. Certainly he or she will not give you the consideration or attention that your presentation needs.

The moral is, by all means, get the name right! It may mean a sale. If you are not sure how a name is pronounced, ask someone else if possible. Otherwise, be honest and apologize. Admit you are not sure how the name should be pronounced and ask someone. That will show you recognize the importance of names and care enough to get them right.

Shakespeare wrote that "a rose by any other name" would "smell as sweet," which is true. However, a prospect called by the wrong name will not respond as sweetly to you! His or her name is as much a part of that person as the nose on the face, perhaps more so. Fortunately, the pronunciation of most names is fairly common and obvious at first glance.

However, when you call on a prospect, do not ask for "Mr. Smith." Personalize your approach by asking for "Mr. Robert H. Smith."

This courtesy should please the prospect because it distinguishes him from all the other Smiths in the directory. Even if the name is listed as Patrick Aloysius McGillicuddy, or something else unwieldy, address him at first approach by the full name.

How To Avoid Offending Prospects

When I call on a prospect, I endeavor to do the things that will please him or her and leave undone the things that might offend, irritate, or aggravate. When I enter an office or home, I remove my hat, if I am wearing one—or an overcoat and overshoes.

As I do not smoke, it is no problem for me to remember to never enter a prospect's domain carrying a lighted cigar, smoking a cigarette, or carrying a pipe. In today's climate, that could offend, irritate, and aggravate, all at once!

Nor do I encounter a prospect with the odor of a particular beverage emanating from my mouth, even if it is only coffee. It pays to ask your spouse or best friend to check your breath from time to time. If you have a bout of bad breath, drinking two glasses of water every two hours daily over the period of a week will ordinarily take care of the problem.

Once in a while, you will run into a prospect who wants to conduct the interview while standing in the door or hall or even behind a desk.

In such a case, I usually say, "Pardon me, Mr. (or Mrs. or Miss) Prospect, this is certainly an imposition as you apparently are busy. I apologize for interrupting you, but can I make an appointment to come back and see you later?"

At this point, the prospect most likely invites me in to sit down. However, one time a prospect continued to ask me questions while standing in the doorway and ignored my request for a later appointment.

Finally I said, "Mr. Prospect, I am sorry, but I have a bone in my leg, and it hurts me to stand on it!"

This old saying brought a grin to his face, and he said, "You win. Come on in."

If a prospect attempts to talk in the presence of another person, I usually say something like this: "Mr. Prospect, I see you are busy. May I come back to see you this afternoon (or in the morning, whichever is applicable)?"

Usually, the prospect understands and excuses the third party or makes a later appointment with me.

Also, I try to make my entrance in a dignified but unassuming way, always thanking the prospect when I am invited to sit down. Courtesy is always appreciated.

The Importance of Courtesy

By way of a digression which actually is pertinent, here is a slant on thoughtlessness that shows a failure in the practice of courtesy in today's society.

I once conducted a personal test to determine how many people still are courteous by holding a door open for twenty different people. The results were that fifteen said nothing, three grunted, and two said "thank you!"

Those two little words do not cost you a cent, but their use can earn dollars for you. Here are a few other things it is important to remember about a prospect:

1. He or she is not dependent upon you, but you on them.
2. The prospect is doing you a favor by listening.

3. The prospect is not just a name but a person.

A prospect is a human being with feelings much like your own. You know what pleases you, so practice on the prospect.

When you run into someone with a "chip on the shoulder," remember the best way to remove it is with a gentle pat on the back. You can always find something about the prospect or his surroundings to praise without sounding as if you are into flattery. Insincerity is usually very detectable.

Avoid being overly familiar. You can make more sales in two months by developing a genuine interest in a prospect than in two years of trying to build their interest in you.

Little acts of courtesy and politeness make a deep impression on the prospect. It is only through this kind of attitude that you can demonstrate a genuine interest in anyone. Courtesy builds an environment of understanding and appreciation that conveys both your desire to be of service and the fact that you have his or her best interests at heart.

The scientific findings that I have discussed in this chapter should help you to establish confidence, win admiration, mold friendship, and influence a prospect to listen to your presentation. Many interviews have been cut short and sales lost because a salesperson failed to apply these principles.

The late Booker T. Washington once said:[1]

> *Success is to be measured not so much by the position that one has reached in life as by the obstacles which he has overcome while trying to succeed.*

---

[1] Washington, Booker T. quoted in God's Little Instruction Book II, (Tulsa: Honor Books, Inc., 1994), p. 9

CHAPTER 13

The Philosophy of Selling

I want to deal with philosophy as it affects you and your relationship to selling. For a more comprehensive understanding of where I am coming from, let me define philosophy:

> *Philosophy comes from the Greek words philo, which means "to love," and sophia, which means wisdom.[1] Therefore, philosophia (philosophy) truly means "the love and pursuit of wisdom."*

Someone has said that philosophy is simply common sense in a dress suit. Actually, common sense is very uncommon. When it is applied, usually it is labeled "wisdom." Wisdom is making wise use of ideas, knowledge, and material things.

What is the most important thing in selling as far as you are concerned? Wisdom's answer is you.

Most men and women fall into two extremes when it comes to considering themselves:

1. Pride, or to think of yourself more highly than you ought, as the Apostle Paul wrote (Rom. 12:3).

2. Or, self-rejection and belittling oneself and one's abilities.

Seldom does anyone see himself or herself honestly or

95

realize what he or she is truly capable of doing. Someone who boasts of his or her own abilities, is cocky or arrogant, and even may show a "false humility." This uses pride as a covering for lack of confidence.

A good salesperson must take stock of himself or herself, honestly analyze capabilities, abilities, and potentiality. Sometimes it takes a friend, spouse, or counselor to see you objectively.

Most of the time, what you think you are is what you are not, and what you think you are not, you may be! Paul finished that admonition with these words: Rather think of yourself with sober judgment (Rom. 12:3).

Mankind is the most wonderful being God ever created, and we remained that even after our first parents' fall from the Garden of Eden. In addition, God gave mankind a mandate: not only to subdue the world, but to replenish it and rule over creation and lower creatures (Gen. 1:28).

Are you aware that you are one of those who has "dominion" over the earth (notice God did not say "dominion over other people")?

You are the being who can think, can comprehend, can co-ordinate and organize, can analyze and visualize, can imagine and dramatize, can see a finished thing from looking at a blueprint.

Most people never think about how amazing it is that only man, of all the creatures on earth, can invent, discover, and construct the marvelous things in the world, especially in the age of technology and electronics.

Can animals harness the forces of nature and turn them into light, power, and heat to make us comfortable? Maybe on "the planet of the apes," as secular scientists and philosophers would like to think, but not on this world.

However, notice that with all the advanced technology, no other worlds as far as the telescope can see are even livable, much less have beings on them. Earth is unique in the universe, and man is unique on earth. You are a unique being. There is not another exactly like you.

You have the faith, the vision, the determination, and the

courage to turn creative ability into sales, to plant ideas that will not only enrich your life but make America a better nation, a better place in which to live.

Self-focus is self-defeating, but getting a true picture of the real you and your place in the world can make you of better service to others.

You can begin this process by sitting down with a note-book and pen or pencil and listing your assets and then your per-sonality liabilities. Build on the one and work on the other to change them to assets.

This process is what enabled me to be confident enough of who I am to talk to thousands of people in all kinds of busi-nesses, all walks of life, all kinds of places, and in all kinds of conditions over the past decades.

During the time I sold tangibles and intangibles by per-sonal solicitation and by direct mail, by letter and by telephone, a great deal of my time went into developing a philosophy of sell-ing.

As I mentioned earlier, a first-hand study of people's actions and reactions has given me insight into their ambitions, aspirations, attitudes, likes and dislikes, and wants and desires, as well as basic human needs.

Knowledge and Experience Become Wisdom

I hope my experience will give you a keener insight into your own ability. Perhaps it will inspire and encourage you to develop more completely your hidden talent of creative selling.

Perhaps reading of what I have learned through knowl-edge and experience will remove a few pebbles out of your path and make the going easier. Anyone can tell you how to sell, but I would like to go beyond that and animate the creative spark in you so that you want to sell.

My philosophy of selling was not garnered by sitting in an "ivory tower" but through becoming a stern realist who faced and met the challenge on the "firing line."

Over more than forty years, I have encountered the problems, the adversities, the conditions, and the situations you will encounter. I have experienced the same heartaches, rejections, and disappointments you will encounter.

Through my experience, I have perhaps solved many of the situations that are perplexing you at this very moment. My philosophy is not based on a "bag of tricks," a few clever sentences, or any other subterfuge that really amounts to "conning" people into buying.

Things (products), words, and people constitute selling.

Therefore, make it your business to study these three things and make a wise use of what you learn in all your activities as a salesperson. My philosophy of selling is based on wisdom, gained through research and experience.

I have touched already in this chapter on the importance of wisdom, but I cannot stress it too much. Wisdom guides you, helps you to discriminate, and gives you the proper suggestions. It enables you to regulate and control your conduct in performing the act of selling.

Wisdom applies sense to selling at all times. Solomon, third king of ancient Israel and known as the "wisest man in the world," wrote: Happy is the man that findeth wisdom and the man that getteth understanding (Prov. 3:13).

Everyone needs wisdom, but in selling, it is a most valuable asset enabling you to get beyond the surface of superficial thinking. It qualifies you to get at the source of things, and that Source is divine intelligence to guide and direct you. Inspiration is the key to creative selling.

The Bible overflows with promises of God's inexhaustible good intended for His creation. The only way to make use of these wonderful promises is to be one with the One who laid them out for us. You can do this by following the instructions in Romans 10:9,10.

King Solomon also wrote: Wisdom is the principal thing; therefore, get wisdom; with all thy getting get understanding (Prov. 4:7).

The man was not talking through his hat! If he lived in America today, there is no doubt he would lead the selling force. Why do I think that? It is because he would get at the root of selling.

He would uncover and search out his own ability for productive and creative thinking and apply those to selling.

He would know that real creative selling does not mean shouting his wares on the street corners.

He would not use hackneyed phrases or bromidic cliches in his presentations.

He would not put prospects into stereotyped categories that are unrealistic.

He would not try to bamboozle or bombard people into buying something against their wills, or something they do not need.

He would know that creative selling is an art that brings the prospect and the product together, an art that guides the prospect into buying that which he needs and that which will give him or her complete satisfaction.

The power of creative selling is a definite means to the end of developing a demand for a product that did not exist before. The need for such selling is greater today in America than it has ever been.

Another proverb is pertinent along these lines: Go to the ant, thou sluggard; consider her ways and be wise (Prov. 6:6).

It is high time for all salespersons to get wise and realize their great potentials and possibilities.

Another valuable lesson to learn from the philosophy of selling is to make spiritual provisions. A salesperson works hard and diligently to make provision for his material comfort. However, he or she needs more than material provisions. There is a need in everyone's life for spiritual provisions.

From material provisions, the body is nourished.

From spiritual provisions, the inner man is nourished, the mind is inspired, and the soul in general is refreshed. This condition helps a salesperson to form a broader concept of self-value and of one's worth to society.

Any prospect can tell whether or not you genuinely respect him or her as a person, not just as a "target," a "mark," or a potential check for you. Every human being likes to be treated with respect and consideration. To convey respect, develop an intense desire to serve a prospect with the best that is in you.

Apply the Philosophy and Get Results

The philosophy of selling trains you to tend your mental garden, to cultivate the idea of living, loving, and sharing, and to develop all your good qualities. As flowers need constant care and good soil in which to thrive, you likewise need to watch your mental garden.

You must uproot the poisonous weeds of selfishness, envy, cynicism, skepticism, jealousy, hatred, distortion, and resentment. These weeds, along with self-rejection, will choke out the good thoughts and ideas.

Instead, you must cultivate kindness, love, consideration for others, gratitude, and appreciation of life and those God brings into your life.

God the Creator loves you as much as any other of His children. Keep reminding yourself of that and make an effort every day to convey this truth to those you meet through your own attitude, personality, and actions.

The world you can see and measure provides physical comforts. The world you can neither measure nor see makes provision for understanding, mental enlightenment, and spiritual discernment.

When you embark on a thought voyage, you give your activity an exalted meaning and your career as a salesperson a broader understanding. From this voyage, you return with a cargo laden with material provision and a reward of genuine satisfaction.

Wisdom encourages you to practice the virtues in life. It is a beacon to illuminate your intelligence, a diadem to place upon your head.

Wisdom makes you earnest, eager, and zestful. The renowned author of the classic Les Miserables, Victor Hugo, wrote that wisdom is the health of the soul.

The salesperson who practices truth and wisdom in his selling activities can gather honey from even a weed. The philosophy of selling teaches a salesperson to live each day fully and completely. This keeps the mind free from worry and a host of mental "vagabonds."

Wisdom enables a person to take things in stride, good or bad. The philosophy of wise selling teaches you not to grieve or worry about the things you do not have and cannot do anything about. It helps you to rejoice and be exceedingly glad about the qualities you do have.

By wisdom, sales are made, and wealth is won. Wisdom teaches you to lose yourself in the service of others, and you will prove the adage that "he profits most who serves best."

I have developed a list of twenty rules by which to live that will keep you from becoming stagnant or bored.

Life's Twenty Rules

1. Compliment three people every day.
2. Watch a sunrise at least once a year.
3. Be the first to say "hello."
4. Live beneath your means; forget about keeping up with the Joneses.
5. Treat everyone as you would like to be treated.
6. Never give up on anyone; miracles do happen.
7. Never deprive someone of hope; it may be all they have.
8. Pray not for things, but for wisdom and courage.
9. Be tough-minded, but tender-hearted.
11. Remember everyone's greatest need is to be appreciated.
12. Keep your promises as if your word is sacred.
13. Show cheerfulness even when you do not feel cheerful.
14. Overnight success usually takes at least ten years.
15. Leave everything better than you found it.
16. Remember that winners do what losers do not want to do.
17. Let the first thing you say of a morning brighten everyone's day.
18. Today you may be a hero to someone; act like it.
19. Find someone to pattern your life after.
20. Ask for help if you need it.

---

[1] Vine, W.E. Vine's Complete Expository Dictionary, (Nashville: Thomas Nelson, Inc., 1984, 1996), "An Expository Dictionary of New Testament Words," p. 470.

CHAPTER 14

How To Close a Sale

Once you have made preparations to approach a prospect, then you need to learn how to close the sale.

One afternoon, when I felt in the prime of sales audacity, or confidence, I approached a well-to-do prospect concerning the purchase of an annuity plan. This plan involved the investment of a substantial amount of money.

I put everything I had into the presentation of that plan. Every phase, every value, and every advantage of what the annuity could mean to him and his family was revealed—visualized, eulogized, and glorified.

At the close of my talk, however, I saw the prospect was attentive but not responsive. He made no move and no comment for the annuity or against it.

Unable to determine his attitude at that point, I retraced the plan, point by point, making a comprehensive summary of each point individually. Finally, getting no response, I simply asked for a check to close the sale. Again, he said nothing.

I thought, "Well, all right, you have not said no and shut the door, and I am not going to do it for you. The only alternative I can see is to `play' your game."

So I sat straight across from him for fifteen minutes during which neither he nor I made a sound. I was determined to wait him out for a "yea or a nay." Finally, he spoke first.

He said, "To whom shall I make out the check?"

When I first considered this man as a prospect, I made plans to close the sale, not just to approach him or to explain the annuity, but to close the sale.

I learned as much about his personality as I could. I discovered his temperament and that he was adamant in his beliefs and his dealings.

It seemed as if it would take three sticks of dynamite to move him. On the other hand, I sensed that "three sticks" might be overkill and ruin the sale. Therefore, in my initial interview I had proceeded to "set off" two sticks, then let silence and quiet close the sale.

The close of a sale is the climax of all selling activity. It is completing the job you set out to do. No sale is a sale without an order. The final step in a successful approach is to close the sale.

When I get to the close of a sale I look at myself as a builder who has constructed a house who has taken time and effort to lay the foundation and erect the walls. The house is complete except for the roof. A sale, up until the time of closing, is essentially a house without a roof.

A contractor certainly would not leave a house in that condition so why should a salesman? If he or she does, in all probability, another builder will step in, put on the roof, and get the pay for the house. A salesperson must hammer until the roof is on, persevere until the sale is closed.

A closing may be easy or difficult, depending on how much thought and preparation a salesperson has devoted to advance planning. Closing a sale is not a tug-of-war or a prize fight but the result of a well-laid plan. The more time spent in preparation, the easier the closing.

If a thorough application has been made of the beginning steps, the ending will be comparatively easy. After all, the close of a sale is the logical conclusion of any interview which has been properly conducted from the moment it began.

At this point, it might be wise to make a complete inventory of your sales technique, reviewing it in the light of the previous chapters of this book.

When you bought this book and began to read it seriously, it became your silent partner. By applying the information in its contents, you will be able to close more sales and increase your earnings.

Making Use of a "Silent Partner"

Although you have not finished reading this book, here are some points to help you make use of the material you have read and the material in the balance of this book.

The chapters on how to attract a prospect and how to create a sale will be of great value in helping you develop positive thoughts and ideas to attract the prospect, anticipate his or her needs and wants, and tailor your appeal to the individual. These two chapters not only detail how to attract prospects but include sound reasons why the prospect should own your product.

The chapter on watching your words will show you how to choose the right words in presenting your proposition, the words that will give the prospect complete understanding of what you are attempting to do for him or her. This will give the prospect full confidence in your presentation.

Have you enthusiasm about your product?

Can you generate this enthusiasm in the prospect? If you feel you have a problem in this area, review the chapter in his "silent partner" on why a prospect buys.

Do you lack insight into how to meet and overcome objections from a prospect? Review the chapter on dealing with objections. Learn how to turn objections into sales.

Are you making full use of your imagination in improving your sales techniques, or are your ideas becoming shop-worn and ragged around the edges?

New ideas about commonplace things often attract attention and arouse buying interest in a prospect. In chapter 22 learn how to turn your imagination into a "junior salesman."

The chapter on the power of personality will help you evaluate your talents, give ideas on how to display your thoughts and ideas, and how to overhaul your speech, voice, and manner—if this "equipment" shows need of polishing or refurbishing.

Do you want to attract more prospects, have the opportunity to close more sales, and extend your sales services? Read the next chapter on how the law of averages can double your sales, if you feel you should be getting paid more for your efforts.

The chapter on the philosophy of selling shows you how

to get honey from a weed! The information in that chapter will undergird your belief that you are offering the prospect the best product on the market.

After this review, we need to look at the question of the right timing in closing a sale.

When To Close a Sale

The right time to close a sale varies of course with the individual prospect. Choosing the right time depends on your empathy with and previous knowledge of the prospect. With some, it might come after five minutes, it might take an hour.

However long it takes, when you sense the prospect yielding, coming into agreement with you, or dropping any objections that have been there, then close the sale.

Whether it has been five minutes or fifty minutes, follow the same procedure.

Do not linger and overstay your prospect's attention span.

Do not talk yourself out of an order you already have obtained.

A well-known figure in the last century wrote of going to hear a missionary talk on his work in a foreign land. At first, the listener was going to write the man a large check. Then as the speaker kept talking, he was going to give him all the money in his pocket. Finally, at the end of the service, this man put a dollar in the offering.

Closing a sale depends on talking enough but not too much.

As you conduct the interview, keep an eye out for "signals." Learn to observe "body language," movements that show the prospect is getting bored or blocking you in some way. Occasionally, ask for the order or make a suggestion leading in that direction. If that does not work, "fire off" the second stick of TNT.

In other words, if your "feelers" do not click, then begin over with something like this: "Mr. Jones, I really feel you do not understand what this plan or product means to you."

Then launch right back into the presentation, calling the

prospect's attention to any particular point that will enable you to stress the value and advantage of your product. If possible, you can cite the opinion of someone this prospect happens to know who has just bought this product and is highly pleased.

As you proceed with your presentation, usually you can determine by the prospect's reactions whether or not he or she has really understood all the value and/or advantages of your product.

If you notice any sign of doubt, ask questions concerning the points which seem to be causing him or her to hesitate. Also, try to think of any possible questions the prospect may have and weave the answers into your presentation.

A good friend of mine, considered to be one of America's top salesmen, has sold enough carpeting to stretch half-way around the world.

He says, "I have never asked for an order in all my experience. My contention is that if I have done a good selling job, there will be no need to ask for the order. The closing takes care of itself."

Another friend with a proven sales record works in a leading Tulsa department store.

She says, "If we approach our customers with sincere interest, they respond in like manner. Not only are they ready to buy, but they will return again and again. A happy customer who can feel the salesperson has a genuine interest in him or her will become a steady customer."

No matter what the terms of your proposition or the kind of product you are selling, you must frame your closing remarks in the most attractive way.

Some Proven Closing Sentences

There are many comments for closing a sale, and they come to you — usually — at the right time, the time when you need them. Some examples are:

"We pay the freight."
"We can set your payment due in 30 days."
"There is an extra percent-discount (whatever percent

your company will allow) for payment on closing."

"Will you be kind enough to let us have your signature?" Or, "Do you write your name Thomas J. Jones or Thomas Joseph Jones? (Never ask a prospect to sign anything, because most prospects do not like the word "sign.")

"What is your wife's full name?"

Salespeople have been "on a roll" at least for the last quarter-century. Those in this profession have had their own ways so long, many have forgotten that the general public is much better informed and wiser than they were before the advent of television commercials.

In many instances, it takes more "selling" than in previous decades in order to close a sale, especially in this era of telemarketers and the irritation they have aroused in many people.

The best and most effective way is to just keep on selling until the prospect says yes. This is the principle which I follow. I feel I have worked honestly and thoroughly to make a sale, and I am not going to leave the door open for someone else if at all possible.

How To Close Sales Effectively

In closing a sale, it is imperative to make your language very plain and simple. Your summary should be complete in every detail and expressed with positive determination. At all times, you should project your belief that every word you have said to the prospects is true and profitable for them.

If possible, when it comes to closing time, have the order blank in one hand and a pen in the other. Help the prospect to say yes.

A salesperson is like the Mississippi, which is made up of many tributaries. Each one contributes its share to the power and strength of the great river.

You are like the river in that you have tributaries of selling qualities, personality attributes, imagination, and experience. Each contributes its share to the power and strength of your salesmanship. The combination of your "tributaries" in full yields the ability to interest prospects and close sales.

Conduct the sale with understanding, consideration, and

appreciation of the prospect. Do not attempt to "bulldoze" or coerce the prospect into closing. Never rush or force him or her against their inclinations.

Exercise tolerance, patience, and a feeling of genuine kindness. If you do the best you can, you will get the sale. On the other hand, if after trying your best, you lose the sale, your efforts will have enhanced the understanding, skill, and power with which you may close the next one.

In closing any sale, insist with tact, plead with earnestness, and persuade with diplomacy. Whatever happens with a sale, do not quit.

Denis Waitley, best-selling author on high-level achievement wrote:[1]

> *Don't wait for that miracle or that break or "the right time." Today is your day. . . . You are in charge of causing your results.*
>
> Don't put it off.
> Don't put your success on layway.
> Don't sit staring at that TV screen letting your mind go blank while you repeat the procrastinator's motto:
>
> I think I can, I think I could; I think I may, I think I should; I think I might, I think I will; I think I better think more still.
>
> Stop rationalizing, get out of your chair, and start doing!

---

[1] Waitley, Denis. The New Dynamics of Winning, (New York: William Morrow and Co., Inc., 1993, Copyright by Nighengale-Conant Corp. and Denis Waitley), p. 32.

CHAPTER 15

The Law of Averages Can Double Your Sales

The Law of Averages is seldom demonstrated as an effective means to help increase sales but is shrouded in mysterious terminology and statistics. All natural laws, which are laws of God, express justice, order, and balance.

Natural laws have no favorites, no special exceptions based on social status, race, gender, or religion. Any so-called "exceptions" to any natural law actually involve a higher law overriding a lower one.

For example, Sir Isaac Newton's observed that items of different weights fall at the same velocity, i.e. a —pound weight and a five pound weight dropped from the same height will reach ground at the same time UNLESS some outside force is applied that causes one weight to be accelerated in its fall.

Natural laws are available to all who apply them, whether they understand them or not, and work in all situations. The law of averages is one of these and can be effectively and efficiently applied to selling. The results can be anticipated with accuracy.

In my decades of experience in the field of selling, I have learned that this law applies the same as in other fields of endeavor. Knowing the effects of this law is one of the most stimulating and fascinating factors in selling. Applying this law guarantees the success of any salesperson.

Let us examine this law in three ways. An understanding of each way will give you a more comprehensive picture of how this law operates. These three are:

1. A practical introduction,
2. An interpretation that will lead to understanding,
3. The application that can double your sales.

As a beginning, or an introduction, take a coin and toss it into the air a hundred times. Mark down the number of times it falls heads and the number of times it falls tails. There are only two sides to that coin and both sides are exposed. The law of averages determines that the coin will fall approximately the same number of times on each side.

The Greek philosopher Socrates used a certain phrase often in beginning a dialogue with someone. "Define your terms."

In my attempt to understand the law of averages, I first tried to define the law, to find a logical interpretation. I wrote letters, made inquiries, and asked questions of many different people and read many different sources. In return, I received many ideas and suggestions.

To sum them up, the answer to understanding the law of averages is: "If you put something in, you get something out." Or, to use Newton's third law of gravity: "Every action has an equal and opposite reaction."

That is a very good answer with an element of truth; however, it did not satisfy me. Many millions of people had seen things fall to the ground before Newton observed the phenomenon in the 17th century and "discovered" the law of gravity.

The difference is that he was the first person to wonder why things of different weights fell at the same speed. (Obviously, this is oversimplified, but this question is what triggered the thinking that resulted in Newton discovering gravity.)

Someone once asked Newton how he discovered this natural law, and he replied, "By thinking about it."

After thinking a long time about the law of averages in terms of application, demonstration, relationships, and results, I came up with the following definition: The law of averages determines the number of times a thing will happen in proportion to the number of times that thing is exposed.

To know a principle, or a law, thoroughly inspires us to apply it. Anyone who applies the law of averages in sales, based on the above definition, cannot fail to produce results.

Many salespeople tend to confuse the law of averages with "luck," or something that happens to you by chance with no rhyme or reason.

Chance, or luck, is gambling that a thing may or may not happen. It is pure risk with a possibility to win something "if your luck holds out." This attitude relieves you of planning, training, or working at success. Usually, with this attitude, you do not have any "luck!"

The cause of a sale is preparation as already explained in this book along with the intelligent application of the law of averages.

A sale might seem to "fall in your lap," and you might attribute it to luck. However, I promise you that somewhere along the way, you planted many ideas about your product and the sale is a delayed reaction of the law of averages.

A certain number of attempts to sell, of planting ideas and knowledge about your product, will result in a certain number of sales averaging out over the long run.

How To Use the Law of Averages

The law of averages leads to or involves two other natural laws: the law of acceleration and the law of compensation.

Set out to sell with a definite goal in view, concentrate on results, and sales begin to take place at an unusual pace. Sometimes, we attribute this to "experience." The more sales you make, the more confidence you have, and even more sales result: the law of acceleration.

The law of compensation never fails to give you results for every ounce of energy you expend. These laws never cheat any man and reward everyone exactly in proportion to the amount of effort they have expended. No one can cheat you but yourself.

The law of compensation embodies the invisible power of

God that guarantees no honest effort toward the right goals with the right motives can result in a loss. Even if the desired result is delayed, your faith is being tested and you are collecting compound interest.

The law of averages operates in all sales activities. It eliminates dependence on luck, ignores chance, fulfills every requirement of successful sales, and allows you to reap the full rewards of its application.

"Ignorance of the law is no excuse" is a maxim in any court in the land. However, sometimes the higher law of mercy comes into play to override justice and allow probation or a lesser sentence. The same principle applies to the laws of creation as to the laws of our land. However, natural laws are more exacting.

Ignorance of the law of gravity will not keep you from falling if you step off a cliff. The fall is not the fault of the law but of your lack of understanding of it.

This principle is expressed in the Bible this way: Whatsoever a man sows that shall he also reap (Gal. 6:7).

In Matthew 13, Mark 4, and Luke 8, the apostles recorded Jesus' teaching on this law in a story called "the Parable of the Sower."

The point was that in order to gain a harvest, a person must sow some seed. Then Jesus explained other "factors" that might override that law: sowing on hard ground, among thorns, or in rocks.

However, if you have good seed, choose your "ground" carefully, prepare it the right way, water and tend the seed, you will harvest a crop. The law of averages will bring a return.

Two other points to remember are that what is reaped will be of the same nature as the seed sowed; and, usually, the crop returns more than was planted.

If you sow the wind, you will reap the whirlwind (Hos. 8:7). If you sow sawdust, you will reap a dust storm.

Many of us, most of the time, are thwarted, distracted, and discouraged because we have no knowledge of the laws on which to base our efforts.

Or, we may know these natural principles but not understand how to apply them in our situations. If so, we are "double-minded," wavering from one goal to another, from one interest to another, and consequently the results of these laws are hindered or even aborted. We end up being simply bewildered or with a suspicion of being cheated.

In applying a fundamental law, do not be anxious or overzealous to change your procedure. Understand that natural laws are unchangeable, do not vacillate, and cannot fail.

Drop whatever is in your hand. Does the law of gravitation kick in? It operates whether you understand it or not, or whether you think of it when you drop something.

All fundamental laws have operated since Creation and can be used if we understand them.

Not many years ago, I had ample opportunity to test the validity of the law of averages in my own field. I was making many calls on the telephone, "casting my line into the water," but not receiving a bite.

Was I dismayed?

Was I frustrated?

Was I discouraged?

Not in the least.

How the Law of Averages Works

I knew the law of averages could not fail, and I knew I was planting the seed of a good life insurance policy that was beneficial to the prospects. I knew my "crop" was growing. I knew results were certain.

What happened? Within a few days, I "hit the jackpot." The last few calls paid off, and I seemed to be inundated with business. In less than a month, I received four dollars for every phone call I had made with a bonus of at least that much more.

The law of averages requires that you approach x-number of prospects, but it does not prescribe how that approach is made. In fact, the law is totally indifferent as to how you "plant your seed."

My personal experience has been that the telephone method is the quickest, most practical, most feasible, and most efficient way of approaching prospects.

The telephone is the fastest method of conveying an idea to the greatest number of people in the shortest period of time. It is the most direct means of exposing an idea in a personalized way and, therefore, fulfilling the requirements necessary for the law of averages to be put into motion.

However you decide to "plant your seeds," to approach your prospects, how many approaches you make determines how many results the law of averages will bring you.

If you sell on a commission, put a definite cash value on each call.

If you work on salary, make an estimate of the number of calls you make in order to consummate a sale.

Keep a record and watch the law of averages at work.

For my records, I place a value of $4 dollars on each telephone call I make and $16 dollars on each personal call. If I make fifty telephone calls in one day or twenty calls in person, I know I have earned $320.

As I said, when I tested this for myself some years ago for a six-month period, I made three thousand phone calls. The law of averages gave me the $4 a call, plus a substantial bonus.

Some readers may wonder about the effect of competition on sales. Actually, I have never given any thought to competition. I was so busy putting the law of averages into operation and availing myself of the opportunities offered me that concern about any competition never entered my mind.

Every call brings a reaction. If it is favorable, act upon it quickly. If it is unfavorable, forget it, and move on to the next call.

In applying the law of averages, it is necessary to learn patience. Nothing about this law promises immediate responses every time, only overall balancing out of sowing and reaping. In the natural world, seeds planted cannot be harvested overnight.

Do not attempt to rush the return. When the apple is ripe, it will fall off the tree. The law of averages cannot be forced, coerced, or hastened. When the requirements are met, it operates with precision. Nothing can make it act or keep it from acting.

The law of averages will remunerate you in proportion to the value you put on it. If you demand little, you will receive little. If you invest a lot, then you will receive a lot. N.W. Ayer, one of the greatest advertising salesmen of his day, had this slogan: "Keeping everlastingly at it brings success."

Some would say this slogan would create "workaholics." I say he was referring to the law of averages. This law does not require a favorable "climate" in which to operate. It will operate for anyone at any time and in any place.

As you approach selling with confidence in the operation of this law, you will find many illuminating thoughts and ideas will come into your mind and a new vista of selling will spread out before you. You will begin to work with the knowledge of unlimited possibilities.

Do not waste time. Those who do are, in essence, throwing away income.

Questions About the Law of Averages

Other questions I have been asked and my answers include these:

Does the law of averages work on a cold canvass? My reply is that there are only hot canvasses!

Does the law of averages work among strangers? My answer is another question, "Does the sun know any strangers? Laws are no respecter of persons."

Does this mean every call results in a sale? No, of course not. It does mean that "on average," you gain as much as you put out.

CHAPTER 16

The Accumulated Value of Sales Effort

Some years ago, I read about a case heard in the British courts based on an ancient law. This case revealed the startling result when things are left to the process of accumulation. The case was Jones vs Smith.

The facts, according to the defendant's counsel, were that his client had agreed, in consideration of a small amount of money, to deliver to the plaintiff two grains of rye on a certain Monday, four on the following Monday, eight on the Monday after, and so on in geometric progression for one year.

The defendant thought he had contracted to deliver only a small amount of grain. However, at the trial, it was shown that all the rye in the world would not be enough to satisfy the obligation. The quantity at the end of the year amounted to 524,288,000 quarters (a quarter being eight bushels or an eighth of a ton). It would have taken more than four billion bushels of rye to satisfy the obligation!

Therefore, in the area of sales, to appreciate the value of accumulated effort, it may be wise to inquire as to its significance. Accumulated effort is gathering or throwing into a "heap" all past performances and experiences. A snowball is a good example of this. The snowball does not roll itself, but when effort is applied it not only rolls but gathers more snow and becomes much larger the longer it rolls.

In selling, a person rolls up a "ball" of experience, for which he or she has paid a definite price in terms of work, studying, energy, time, and effort. Both physical and mental energy have been expended, also emotional.

This experience is of value, and you want to make every effort to utilize it, to begin the roll of a small snowball into a large "boulder" or heap of snow. You want to see the accumulated results manifest.

How To Utilize Accumulated Experience

There are three steps in the utilization of accumulated selling experience to best advantage: Keep complete records, carry out periodical reviews, and **keep complete records.**

All businesses have some system of accounting that coordinates all departments into a whole. All transactions are detailed and recorded. Businesses that do not keep accurate records or that keep sloppy accounts will run into trouble sooner or later, probably with the Internal Revenue Service!

However, in this area, I am talking of keeping complete records, not just for your accountant but for your own knowledge of what you are doing. In a large enough business, an audit is done every few months, not only to check each department but to compare them with one another. A balance is struck, in other words.

It is easy to determine success or failure of each part of the business, as well as of the whole. Many businesses are saved from total failure and/or make financial progress by a running check of these figures.

As a salesperson, your business may not be large enough to require a full-scale accounting system. However, you must have a system of some kind to keep a complete record for taxes and to see whether you are succeeding.

Every call, every appointment, and every interview has value and should be recorded, along with the results of each. Any other information that might be helpful to you in the future in return calls or in elimination of prospects or in calls on other prospects should also be recorded.

Carry out periodic reviews

Each month, set aside time to review each incident and examine thoroughly your performance in each instance and the results. This will help develop a method of analyzing your efforts and improving past performances. You might call this rolling up the first small snowball. Your experience also will be broadened, just as the snowball is each time it rolls over.

Evaluating your experience, then visualizing it in conjunction with your creative ability will generate enthusiasm and automatically produce more sales. Your "summing up" will encourage you to greater efforts.

In your reviews, ask yourself these questions:

What was the outcome of the last call on this prospect?
What was his or her reaction—favorable or unfavorable?
What caused this reaction? My product or my presentation?
What suggestions did I make that were received?
What suggestions were not received, and why?
What was included or omitted that made a difference?
What impression did I make on the prospect?
What was the reason given for postponing the sale?
Was it valid or feigned, and why?

In making these analyses, you will uncover many hidden ideas and suggestions that will help you in a return call or with the next prospect. Also, you will find your enthusiasm and confidence increased, like that snowball.

A gold mine is a concentration of that precious metal in one spot underground. Those deposits are of no value unless they are found, mined, and refined for sale or use. The finished product results from the application of effort and thought. You have a gold mine in the form of stored-up records of past experiences.

A little thought and effort will enable you to "mine" these deposits of experience. An old saying is that to get something done quickly, give it to the busiest person you know. Why is this true in most instances? It is because that person has learned to evaluate his or her time and use it efficiently.

Therefore, as a salesperson, learn to use your time efficiently if you are not already doing that. It will amaze you what can be done in a short period of time with experience, organization, and effort. A salesperson renders a service to others as well as financial rewards to himself. Every constructive thought toward the completion of a sale is a contribution toward that service.

Perfecting selling as a public service can be advanced through the kind of retrospection I have been describing in this chapter. As you review, you can see the value of patience, diligence, sincerity, alertness, and kindness. You will see the value of honesty and a genuine desire to help others.

Looking at your sales experience in retrospect will make you more aware of your responsibility to prospects, more considerate of them, and more loyal to your "calling." Therefore, your review and evaluation of past performances and experiences will help you earn more money and develop better plans for the future.

Turn accumulated efforts into cash

The hardest and most trying task in selling is to find "live" prospects. Selling is comparatively easy once the target is found, although there always are those who do not buy even after all your efforts. If you have been in sales any length of time, you have a list in your records of prospects who have not become clients.

Experience has shown you how to approach them and, probably, how not to. You know something about each one. However, for one reason or another, you have been unable to consummate the sale. Do not give up! Try again. Sometimes, what you think is "chaff" really is wheat, just not yet ripe. What you considered only a potential or possibility may yet be a sale.

By reviewing and properly evaluating your experiences, something new will always be uncovered that will give you a fresh approach. In our present climate of capitalism, economic, political, and social changes come about so quickly that a person who yesterday was a possibility may today be a "live" prospect.

For example, in a hundred old prospects, you might easily find new sales in a fourth of them. Remember in the last chapter we saw how the law of averages eventually compensates you for honest effort? However, also remember that patience must play a part. The averages "average out" over a period of time, not always immediately.

Every prospect you have approached represents an investment of knowledge, skill, time and effort. That investment has a definite cash value, but you are the only one who can reap the benefits. By evaluating past prospects and deciding to "try, try again," you may uncover one who will become a best customer. This has happened to me a number of times.

Once a prospect was buried so deep in my files that his card had turned yellow. Then I decided to take another "run" at him—and it paid off. I made one of the best sales of my entire career. Do not abandon ship although it seems to be sinking.

A Hypothetical Example of Accumulation

If Christopher Columbus in 1492 had deposited one dollar in the Bank of America at 4 percent interest compounded annually, that one would have snowballed into enough dollar bills to reach around the world twice.

It will pay you to transfer the dormant ideas of accumulated experience from the Bank of Past Performances to an active account in the Bank of Sales Completed.

It is not what you know about selling that counts—although that is extremely important as a beginning—but what you do with what you know.

Once I drove past the federal prison in McAllister, Oklahoma. Seeing the high walls, iron-barred windows, and armed guards at the huge gates, my heart went out in pity for the men confined there, although they were there through their own choices and actions.

As I was giving thanks I could walk the earth a free man, the question occurred as to how free I really was.

Most of us are not imprisoned behind walls of mortar and bars of iron, but we live in "prisons" of the mind and personality. Instead of iron, we live behind invisible "walls" of fear, discouragement, lack of self-esteem and self-confidence, bitterness and resentment, unforgiveness, and worry.

Many people have a stronger faith in what they cannot do than in what they can do. Our "walls" are built by negative faith. We are our own jailers, locking ourselves in cells of unhappiness and failure behind iron bars forged through wrong choices, inertia, and pessimism (negative faith).

Fortunately, there is one shining ray of hope about most of our "prisons." We have the key to escape. That key is positive faith that reverses all the invisible "walls" that hinder us in developing our personalities to their full, positive expression.

> *Stone walls do not a prison make,*
> *Nor iron bars a cage.*[1]

---

[1] Lovelace, Richard [1618-1658] from Familiar Quotations by John Bartlett, 1882, (Boston: Little, Brown and Company), 14th printing of the 13th and Centennial Edition, Revised, 1955)

CHAPTER 17

The Power of Personality

The 15th Century artist Leonardo Da Vinci was once asked what he was painting, and he answered, "Souls." Others painted faces and bodies, but he wanted to portray the inward being through outward features. He wanted to capture the real person, not the "suit of clothes" (body of a person).

I like to think he was painting the personality of his subject. People have been known to stand for hours before his famous painting, the Mona Lisa, trying to understand the essence of the painting.

What is personality? It is the essence of a person, the mind, emotions, and will expressed in how a person thinks, feels, and behaves.

Some say it is the extent to which an individual has developed habits and skills that may be used to interest and serve not only their own needs but others.

Some call personality "the social-stimulus value" of each individual.

I like to think that personality is an attribute that flows out of one's consciousness, an outward synthesis of the inward intensity of thinking, feeling, and being.

Personality is the "powerhouse" that generates the "electricity" that lights up and powers the individual. This "powerhouse" generates the power to serve the needs of those around you.

You are a dynamic organism composed of many different qualities and attributes. The more harmoniously your parts work together, the more power can flow through your personality.

As a salesman, you want to develop and enlarge the essence of yourself that reflects through your eyes, your voice, and your manner. This can be accomplished by improving the expressing of your personality.

Personality might be said to reflect one's character. So, then, what is character? Webster's Dictionary defines character in this sense as:

> *¹Essential quality, nature, kind, or sort; the pattern of behavior or personality found in an individual or group . . . moral strength, self-discipline, fortitude, etc."*

Character is what you really are, and personality is what people see and perceive you to be. Ideally, your character is an integral part of your personality. Otherwise, you become hypocritical, at least somewhat phony and shallow, and what the Bible calls "double-minded" (James 1:8).

Some say character is a combination of habits acquired over a long period of time, both good and bad. However, I say your habits simply reflect your character. All habits are acquired through choices, an act of will. An old saying is that repeating anything three times causes it to become a habit!

How To Change Your Character

Building character begins in the home. It continues through the educational process of church and school. Then character is finalized or firmed up in adulthood via choices as to how one meets and deals with experiences.

An important thing to remember is that character can be changed, thus changing one's personality.

You can discard any habit and form new ones. You not only have the right to choose, but you have the responsibility. Only you are accountable for the kind of character and personality you have. No matter how good or bad your childhood was, once you are an adult, you can change any "programs" that influence your life.

All habits of behavior or attitude (patterns of thinking) can be improved or discontinued and replaced. In the field of sales, it lies within your domain to develop the traits of character that will allow you to better serve your prospects.

Creative selling offers you an unparalleled opportunity to develop your personality, fine-tune your character, and at the same time, reap material rewards as well. The impression you make on others is a product of many factors, large and small. Therefore, strict attention and careful consideration must be given to the "powerhouse" that produces the impression.

Five Steps To Overhauling Your "Powerhouse"

I have discovered five steps to "overhauling one's powerhouse." They are to analyze present habits, rely on yourself, develop optimism, stay in motion, and develop patience.

• Analyze your present habits

No one knows the real truth about your conduct, behavior, and habits better than you. No one is better qualified than you to analyze and correct them. Know your faults, then you can set out to replace them with assets.

The best way to approach this is to make an honest evaluation of yourself:

How many everyday habits do I practice that are useful?
What is my overall motive in life?
Do I put my interests and welfare ahead of others?
Can I judge the effect of my behavior on other people?
Can I set aside my own feelings to see others' feelings?
How good am I at getting along with others?
Do I have confidence in my own abilities?
Do I examine things I hear to make up my own mind?
Am I covetous, envious, jealous, and self-centered?
Do I practice saying "thank you" and "please"?
Then, do the same thing with your approach to prospects:
What is my attitude toward the prospect as well as toward myself?
Are my thoughts and actions positive?

Am I tolerant and considerate of the prospect?

Do I honestly respect his or her opinions?

Do I interrupt him while he is speaking?

Do I permit objections to deter my real mission?

Do I monopolize the conversation with a big "I"?

Am I arrogant or rude, seeing a prospect as "little you"?

Am I persistent without being offensive or "pushy"?

Do I float like a thistle from opinion to opinion?

Conscious effort to improve the impression you make on prospects by genuinely developing good character traits will pay off in all areas of your life.

Rely on yourself

As you begin to be more self-reliant, you will develop many hidden traits of character and find more natural abilities. Your ability to evaluate and meet any situation will improve. After all, no two fingerprints are alike, nor are any two personalities exactly alike. You cannot imitate another's fingerprint, so why try to imitate another's personality?

Train yourself to rely on your mental resources, judgment, and abilities. Develop integrity and have faith in your own character. Think, speak, and act on your convictions, and that will influence a prospect. Act as if it is impossible for you to fail.

You will run into situations where conditions must be met on the spot with no time or way to rely on anyone else. You must know instantly when to smile, when to frown, when to talk and when to keep quiet, when to move and when to sit still. All of this knowledge will affect the prospect.

Self-reliance develops character. To perfect yourself is to perfect your selling ability.

Develop optimism

Look for the best, expect nothing but the best, and you will always share the best. Optimism is thinking straight, an excellent vaccine to prevent failure. Optimism will help you to maintain your emotional equilibrium, regardless of what happens.

A graphic description of the effect of an optimistic attitude is the old saying: When you walk toward the light, the shadows are in back of you; when you walk away from the light, the shadows are in front of you.

Practice and demonstrate optimism in your selling, and you will always be walking toward the light. The prospect has troubles of his or her own, and an attitude of optimism can also help to lift those for the prospect as well as keep you on an even keel.

Stay in motion

Sales follow action. When intelligently directed, each sale is one step closer to the next one. Keep active, and you will soon get there. Everything in nature is always active, in motion from this stage to the next. Bees are active, ants are active, even the cells in your body are active.

It is more fun to wear out than rust out. Another adage is also true: Do not let the grass grow under your feet if you want to get somewhere. When you keep on the move, you advance.

If you have a tendency toward pessimism, list that in your character analyzation. Begin to turn it around by thinking positively. Defeat will turn into achievement. So "all things come to him who waits?" However, you do not have to stand still while you wait—keep moving forward.

Develop patience

Remaining in motion does not mean being impatient. Motion or action that leads to an advance is a patient, consistent, confident process.

Patience implies composure, self-confidence, and self-assurance without arrogance and pride.

Patience realizes that all conditions and situations are only temporary. If you remain "calm, cool, and collected," the most trying situation will work itself out.

Patience teaches us "to grin and bear it," because things will change sooner or later.

Patience sees trials, tribulations, troubles, obstacles, delay, disappointments, and failures as temporary roadblocks.

Patience utilizes the times spent waiting to see prospects by reading something that will add to your knowledge or your life in some way.

There are many details in the creative-selling field, and patience is one way to master those details. Every task begins and ends in details. In mastering all these details, patience will be your biggest help.

Putting these five suggestions into action will change your character, and your personality will reflect these changes. Your "powerhouse" will operate more harmoniously and with greater success.

The longer I live, the more I realize the impact of attitude. Attitude, to me, is more important than facts, more important than money, circumstances, successes or failures, or than what others say or do to or about you. It is more important than appearance, talent, or abilities.

Attitude will make or break a company . . . a church . . . a home. The remarkable thing is that each person has a choice every day about what attitude he or she will approach life with that day.

We cannot change our pasts.

We cannot change how other people act.

We cannot change the inevitable in events.

The only way we can influence immediate events around us is by our attitudes. I am convinced that 10 percent of our lives is what happens to us, and 90 percent is how we react to it.

You are in charge of your attitude, and attitude is everything! Choose to be happy and those you are around or whom you meet will be more apt to react to you in a positive way.

Sixteenth-century poet Sir Henry Wotton wrote about the character of a happy life this way:[2]

> *How happy is he born and taught,*
> *That serveth not another's will;*
> *Whose armor is his honest thought,*
> *And simple truth his utmost skill!...*
> *Who hath his life from rumors freed,*

Whose conscience is his strong retreat;
Whose state can neither flatterers feed,
Nor ruin make oppressors great.

---

[1] Webster's New World Dictionary, Third College Edition, (New York:
Prentice Hall, a Macmillan Company, 1986), p. 235.
[2] Bennett, William J., Ed. The Book of Virtues, (New York: Simon &
Schuster, 1993), p. 619; "The Character of a Happy Life," by Sir Henry
Wooton.

CHAPTER 18

How To Develop Your Power of Expression

A large percentage of a salesperson's time is spent in expressing ideas. It will pay large dividends to improve the mechanics of expression: your speech, your voice, and your manner.

Speech is the ability to utter sounds and/or words, to express ideas and thoughts in words. Good speech involves enunciating clearly, unhurriedly, and distinctly in order to most efficiently get your ideas across to the prospect.

By patiently examining your speech patterns, you can correct any weaknesses or habits that hinder your ideas from being not only understood but received.

A prospect judges you by what you say, as well as by your appearance. He or she only understands what you say about your product, not yet having tried it out. Train yourself to speak plainly and with dignity. Pronounce each word carefully and distinctly.

Speech, voice, and manner are all fundamental parts of your expression. How you use those factors affects your ability as a salesperson. Those three attributes express your personality. They tell the prospect who you are as well as what you are selling.

However, what you say and how you say it—your

speech—is expressed through the medium of your voice. An unpleasant, harsh, strident, or otherwise negative voice will make of no affect the right speech, a good personality, the best product, and a great creative sales pitch.

If you have a speech defect or a voice problem, you can always seek out a voice coach, as film actors and actresses do. Without the right voice tones and patterns, none of them would be a success. In fact, when sound was first added to silent movies, a few of the until-then most famous stars no longer were able to be used in films. Their voices made tragedies into comedies!

There are some things you can do, however, without resorting to voice coaches. First, make a tape of your presentation or of yourself reading something. Then listen to that tape over and over, critiquing it as if the voice belonged to someone else.

Something as simple as practicing deep breathing can improve the tone of your voice. Breathing regulates and controls the tone, the pitch, and the inflection of your voice. Taking a few deep breaths before entering the office or home of a prospect adds to the effect of your voice.

As a matter of fact, deep breathing also helps your health. It strengthens your lungs, adds oxygen to your blood, and adds to a general feeling of well-being.

Another thing that will help is reading a few pages of something out loud every day. Take a dictionary and pronounce some words aloud, trying to enunciate each syllable clearly and distinctly. This only takes a few minutes a day, but soon you will see a great improvement in your voice.

Saying the multiplication tables out loud will improve the sound, volume, and resonance of your voice. This takes about four minutes and, if repeated several times a week, also will bring an improvement to your voice and speech.

As all words are formed from letters, another simple aid is to speak the alphabet aloud several times a week, giving each letter the full use of lungs and diaphragm. Note the different formations of your mouth as you say each letter out loud.

Once you have strengthened your voice and worked for a while on your enunciation and voice tone, then you can work on achieving clarity in your speech.

How To Achieve Clarity in Your Speech

Stand in front of a mirror and carry out some of the exercises I just mentioned. See if you open your mouth wide enough when you speak. Not doing so causes your words to be slurred and not clear. By observing yourself talking aloud, you will train out any drawl or sloppy enunciation from your voice.

If you hear on the sample tape that you do drawl some words, practice changing this by watching yourself say each syllable of the words with which you have trouble. Take the words apart as most words are made up of more than one syllable. Then speak each part of the word clearly and distinctly until you no longer slur that word when you speak.

Make it easy for a prospect to understand what you are talking about. Express your ideas clearly and distinctly, and they will turn more easily into sales. Clarity of speech is very important. Cultivating the habit of perfecting your voice and speech will pay off in great dividends.

It also will pay to learn not to hurry in your presentation. Clear, understandable speech depends on speaking unhurriedly. Know your presentation thoroughly, and deliver your talk distinctly in a relaxed manner, and what you say is more persuasive, more effective, and more convincing.

If you do this, usually it will not be necessary to repeat any of your presentation. This saves time for both you and the prospect. It may also save you some embarrassment. Breathe evenly and pause at proper intervals. Do not try to speak a whole paragraph with only one breath. That makes you sound unprofessional.

In addition, clarity depends on your tone of voice. Develop a calm, conversational tone. A "pushy" or, the opposite, a weak tone, detracts immensely from your presentation. The wrong tone also can offend or irritate the prospect, and your sale will fly out the window.

Courtesy, appreciation, kindness, and thoughtfulness are sometimes considered "little" things. Yet those very things loom large in communicating with others. Just think of the people you like to listen to and figure out why.

The best personality in the world is no good to you or

anyone else unless you can communicate well.

Learn to leave your troubles outside the prospect's door. A melancholy feeling will be communicated to whoever hears you. No matter how sad you are, how worried, or even, how angry, learn to separate your emotions from your presentation.

These may seem like little things, but they make a whale of a difference. Remember to smile as you talk. This tells the prospect that you like him, that you want to help him or her, and it makes you feel better as well as the prospect. It is very hard to smile and hang onto any of those negative emotions.

Express Your Personality in a Smile

A smile in your voice unlocks doors, creates a friendly atmosphere, and helps people believe in you as well as like you. Most people will respond to a friendly smile and a pleasant voice. Relax, smile and feel kindly toward a prospect, be yourself, and in all probability you will leave the office with a sale and, perhaps, a new friend.

Courtesy, graciousness, and friendliness are valuable assets in any area of your life. Remember that your speech, your voice, and your manner are you. They are the vital qualities of your personality. They are you in action.

You can make them mechanical and ineffectual through not showing personal interest. On the other hand, you can make them human, brimful of personal interest and charm. You can express thoughts and ideas that will persuade and motivate.

Dramatize your speech, voice, and manner with imagination, enthusiasm, and color. The "magic power of personality" is the intensity of thinking, feeling, and being. It is the harmonious action of all the different mechanisms of the powerhouse we talked about in the last chapter.

Expressing yourself favorably overcomes objections and subdues arguments. It produces an effect on the prospect that impels action. It is the magnet that draws the prospect to you. Developing clarity in speech and a pleasant voice and learning how to express yourself to the best advantage is like finding a gold mine. So give a smile!

A smile costs nothing but gives much. It enriches those who receive without making poorer those who give.

A smile takes but a moment, but the memory of it sometimes lasts forever.

A smile is something no one is so rich or mighty that he or she can get along without; nor is anyone so poor but that a smile will add riches.

A smile creates happiness in the home, fosters good will in business, and is the symbol of friendship.

A smile brings rest to the weary, cheer to the discouraged, sunshine to the sad.

A smile is nature's best antidote for trouble.

A smile cannot be bought, begged, borrowed, or stolen for it is of no value to anyone until it is given away.

A smile is of great value to those too tired to smile themselves. No one needs a smile as badly as someone who has no more smiles of his or her own.

Along with a smile, watch the kind of words you speak.

Watch Your Words

I once read about a test conducted to measure the vocabularies of certain groups of individuals. These groups included top executives of successful corporations, graduate engineers, liberal arts college graduates, and college professors. The test was based on 150 words and definitions.

The results were as follows: the engineers averaged 120 correct definitions, the liberal arts graduates averaged 129, college professors averaged 142, while the executives averaged 143. These executives had gotten to their top positions in large part because of an ability to sell ideas to their associates.

In order to do this, they must have developed an extensive and accurate vocabulary. They had to be able to choose the correct word for a certain thought at the right time.

One of the most potent tools in a salesperson's kit is a good vocabulary.

Words are "tools" to describe, define, explain, illustrate, and cause a prospect to visualize a product.

Words open the interview and close the sale. Therefore, it is wise to concentrate on developing a vocabulary that will increase word power and make selling more effective.

Any salesperson can accomplish this by devoting a few minutes each day to the suggestions outlined in this chapter. Understand that your vocabulary is extremely important in sales.

As a salesperson, you do not need the vocabulary of an anthropologist, for example, but you do need to know words that add color and depth to your presentation of a product. A group of words of this nature will qualify you to portray the advantages and benefits the prospect will derive from your product.

Knowing the derivation, meaning, correct usage, and definition of any word you use will increase your ability to communicate to a prospect and your confidence in your product and in your ability to sell it.

Get the "dictionary habit." Look up any word you read or hear of which you do not already know the meaning and the correct pronunciation. Reader's Digest magazine has a section each month listing several words and their correct meanings and pronunciations. This is a fun and easy way to add to your vocabulary.

Using these tests and adding words of your own could mean that at the end of a year you could have hundreds of new words. I have figured that each word will be worth at least $2, adding as much as $1,000 a year.

Another fun and easy way to increase your word power is by working crossword puzzles. Start with easy books or the ones in daily newspapers and work up to the difficult New York Times puzzles!

In the United States, there are about 300 million people, all of whom are susceptible to the power of words. Words move, impel, and influence. A salesperson who has command of a good "stock" of words is the one who takes the lead and picks the choicest plums in the field of selling.

People respond more quickly, studies show, to the spoken word than to the written word. Spoken words are sounds that touch the prospect's basic nature and are a sure means of getting the quickest reaction and the most favorable response. Spoken words even outrank pictures and color in getting reactions.

Ideas first appear as words in the mind, which we then call thoughts. It is essential to use the best ones at the right time. Therefore, we ought not to take words or our spoken language for granted. Think about it for a minute: Just what is a word?

Webster's says a word is "a speech sound or series of them, serving to communicate meaning" or "a unit of language."[1]

140

Beyond those definitions, a word is:

A definite unit of intelligence,

A symbol for some thing (human, animal, vegetable, or mineral), some thought or idea, or some theory or philosophy,

An utterance implying the belief or authority of the one who says it.

Without meaning, the sounds coming from one's mouth are just noises. Animals make noises; people "noises" are words.

A salesperson employs sounds with meaning to convey a message to a prospect. To do this successfully, you must think out your ideas in a reasonable way that will mean something to the prospect.

You might say words are the wings of thought, so choose words that make your thoughts fly.

There are really only two ways of communication between people who can see and hear: the spoken word and the written word. To make either method more vivid and effective, it is important to know good grammar and how parts of speech fit together as well as having a good vocabulary.

Five "Master-Key" Words

Every industry abounds with certain key words. Most industries are built around those words. A key word can be compared to a master key that unlocks an entire building.

The master key to the Empire State Building is tiny in comparison to the building itself, taking up only a small space in someone's pocket. Yet it permits a complete inspection of the huge structure.

In the same way, words are keys to unlock all the doors of knowledge about your product. The right "keys" will give a prospect a comprehensive view of your product's advantages. A salesperson actually has five master-key words: describe, explain, define, illustrate, and visualize.

To describe your product, select the best words to introduce its advantages to the prospect. Here is where the parts of speech called "adjectives" and "adverbs" come into play. Learn to describe your product in concise yet colorful words.

To explain means to make something plain. Begin by

making your product plain to yourself. Describe it to yourself in a way that will explain what it means to the prospect, what it can do for him or her, and how it works.

If you can describe the product and explain it in a way that would cause you to buy it, then you can get its benefits across to a prospect.

To define your product, understand that a precise definition of one word distinguishes it from all other words. Even with synonyms, usually one word will better fit the particular item or situation than another. Look up in a dictionary any words not familiar to you, so that you can define everything about your product accurately.

To illustrate means to enlighten the prospect and illuminate your product. A chart, a picture, a map, or some other visual means may add to your description in words. Some people learn through hearing; others through visualization. By paying close attention to the prospect as you talk, you can see which method of communication will reach him or her best.

To visualize means to present your information to a prospect in such a way that he or she can form a mental image of the product and its benefits. Creating a mental picture of your product in the prospect's mind goes a long way toward closing a sale.

I have selected five different industries to illustrate the principle of the five "master key" words listed above.

First of all, let us look at the steel industry. Steel is a cold, hard-sounding word, yet the product is formed by heat. There are three key words associated with this industry: crucible, tensile, and durable. A crucible steel is one formed by fusing iron, carbon, and flux in a special "pot" (a crucible). Tensile means "capable of steel," one resistant to stress, able to stretch and bend without doing injury to its own "muscles." Durable, of course, means "able to endure." This kind of steel is long-lasting and can withstand the wear and tear of the elements.

Secondly, take the oil industry's three master words: lubrication, density and viscosity. Lubrication reduces friction, increases efficiency, lengthens the life of any machine, and lessens costs. The density of oil determines its thickness — light, medium or heavy. Viscosity determines the wearing quality of an oil. This factor determines the ability of an oil to withstand friction.

The third industry to consider is the paint, roofing and allied industries. The three key words to describe one of these products include waterproofing, which prevents leaks and preserves interiors; protection, the factor of the product that keeps surfaces intact; and anti-corrosion, which prevents the chemicals in the air from eating away the surface of the paint, roof, or whatever. This element stops disintegration or deterioration.

As a fourth example, look at the household appliance industry. Customers want convenience, comfort and economy. A salesperson would use these three words to convey how the product is efficient and easy to maintain; how it gets things done with the least amount of effort, giving the user more time for other things and enhancing his or her comfort; and how the price is economical compared to what the product will accomplish.

The above four industries involve tangible products. Let us look now at an industry involving an intangible product: life insurance. The three key words here are estate, savings, and income. Life insurance creates an immediate estate in case of the death of the insured, allowing him or her to "build" an estate on the installment plan. Savings come in with the type of life insurance that can be cashed in or borrowed on before the insured person's death. Income will derive from a life-income insurance plan.

Using the three key "master words" for any industry allows a salesperson to describe, explain, define, illustrate and cause a prospect to visualize a product. Look at your product and see which three words give you the ability to do these five things, completely communicating the value of your product to a prospect.

How To Use Words Effectively

A lot of words thrown together may only be noise, but if used in the right combination and spoken with the right pitch and tempo, they become notes and tones of power, "master keys" to sales. A carpenter would not attempt to drive a nail with a saw or cut with a hammer.

A mathematician cannot do math without numbers, a musician cannot make music without notes, and a salesperson will not reap any sales without the right words. The moral is increase your word power. I once made a $2,500 life insurance sale with a hundred simple words detailing the difference between "insurance" and "assurance."

When a salesperson successfully carries his or her point to a prospect in the right words, there is a meeting of minds, an understanding, and usually, an agreement.

I have found that, in selling, it is best not to use words of several syllables, technical phrases not familiar to the average person, and "jargon" that those in your industry use but outsiders do not. This kind of language usually amounts to "sound and fury" but "signifies nothing," so your sale goes down the drain instead of flying.

Which of the following sentences is more likely to produce the greatest response and convey the most meaning? "The spectacular conflagration was caused by the instantaneous combustion of phosphorus," or "The fire was caused by a match"?

Therefore, in developing your creative sales presentation, study and analyze each word you use. Find out if what you are saying is being understood the way you meant it. Make sure the words you use are the right tools to get the idea from your mind to the prospect's.

It will pay you to use plain, simple, well-known, "everyday" words with meanings most people understand. Your words are the only means a prospect has of understanding your product.

Increasing your word power will mean increasing the money in your pocket. To sum up the information in this chapter: analyze yourself, analyze your selling position, analyze your product, analyze your vocabulary and each word you use in your sales plan. Ask yourself whether the words you use appeal to you.

Would they make you act?

Would they convince and persuade you to buy your product?

If so, your words probably will have the same effect on a prospect. Learn not to present your sales plan like a parrot or a robot.

Now that you have overhauled your personality and developed a great vocabulary, in the next chapter let us discuss the beginning of how to make actual sales. That is by making appointments to see prospects.

Some kinds of sales utilize door-to-door approaches or dropping into an office unannounced and unexpected. Perhaps that works in some cases.

However, if you are selling a good product from a reputable company, the professional approach is to call ahead and make a definite appointment to see a prospect at a definite time. This is the best use of your time as well as the prospect's.

Above all, do not stop trying. Success in selling comes to those who believe they cannot be defeated as long as they do not quit. Those are the salespeople who end up victorious.

<u>Victory</u>

You are the man who used to boast that you would achieve the uttermost - someday. You merely wished a show, to demonstrate how much you know and prove the distance you can go . . . .

Another year we have just passed through. What new ideas came to you? How many big things did you do? Time . . . left twelve fresh months in your care. How many of them did you share with opportunity and dare again where you so often missed?

We do not find you on the list of Makers-Good. Explain the fact! Ah, no, twas not the chance you lacked! As usual—you failed to act![2]

---

[1] Webster's, p. 1538.

[2] Bettger, p. 9.

CHAPTER 20

How To Make Appointments

Efficiency is the capacity to produce desired results. It is the effective operation of a business or performance of a business task with minimum of wasted effort. It is getting maximum results with minimum effort, the application of thought to action.

Efficiency is the application of common sense, the act of doing the right thing at the right time. In selling, efficiency is the ability to make the greatest number of sales with the least possible amount of effort in the shortest period of time.

Various sales managers and executives have estimated that the average salesperson spends only about two hours working time each day actually interviewing prospects. The rest of the time is spent in getting from place to place or in calling on prospects who are not available, which is an inefficient use of time.

A salesperson does not get paid for wasting time, but for using his time efficiently. The best way to get your proposition in front of a prospect while saving your time and conserving your energy is to make an appointment. In the long run, that is much more efficient than the trial and error of attempting to catch up with prospects without an appointment.

What is an appointment? It is an arrangement for a meeting, laying the groundwork for an interview, preparation for seeing a prospect face to face in order to present your sales plan.

Actually, it is putting you in a place before you literally get there. Make an appointment, and you eliminate a disappointment!

A great number of salespeople sell products that require a demonstration at the prospect's place of business or home, or at the salesperson's place of business, or perhaps at some other convenient place.

A lot of time and energy can be saved, as well as more money made, if part of the selling time each day is spent in making definite appointments.

Three Methods of Getting Appointments

There are three main ways of making appointments, particularly with prospects with whom you have not become previously acquainted. That is by mail, by referral, or by telephone.

To make appointments by mail, first write the prospect a brief letter stating the time you would like to see him or her and the purpose of the interview. The letter should be brief but cordial and include something to pique the interest of the prospect.

The letter should be sent at least two days ahead of the time you want the appointment, not so far ahead that your request could be forgotten but far enough in advance to ensure the prospect could have some unscheduled time open.

If you know someone who also knows your prospect, ask your friend or acquaintance to write a note on his or her personal business card introducing you. Usually, as a courtesy to someone already known to the prospect, an appointment will be set up.

Alternatively, this friend-in-common might make a telephone call on your behalf, vouching for you.

However, the most effective method of making appointments is by your own use of the telephone as a medium of communication. Make the telephone your "junior salesperson." An hour each day or even half an hour will greatly improve your efficiency, enlarge your opportunities, and add substantially to your income.

In order to do this successfully, here are a few steps that will help: organize your thoughts, your list of prospects, and your words of approach. Then make a definite appointment.

In other words, work up a plan of action by deciding in advance what you will say to the prospect. When you get a prospect on the phone, tell him in plain, concise words what you want to do for him in an interview.

When you see the prospect, remind her or him of your phone conversation, amplify what you said, prove the merits of your product so that the prospect will feel the need for it, get the order, and then leave. Do not wear out your welcome.

Suppose I am a salesman representing the fictitious Monitor Company of California, manufacturers of textile specialties. I have been assigned to Philadelphia, where I have never been and where my company has never sold a single product up to now. In fact, the company is not known in Pennsylvania except through trade papers.

I am a stranger in a strange territory, selling a product strange to the public from a strange company. How am I going to even get started? First, I turn to the classified advertising section of the city telephone directory and find a list of firms in my field.

What an opportunity! However, remember that in addition to my other "handicaps," I know nothing about any of these companies. I do know that a hosiery firm, for example, would not generally buy textile specialties. However, I do know that someone in the ABC Hosiery Company might be in charge of buying such specialties.

So I call the firm's receptionist or switchboard operator and ask for the person who buys "spindle threaders." She tells me that is "Mr. Buck," so I ask to be connected to him. When he answers his phone, I tell him quickly but clearly who I am, what company I represent, and how our products can increase his firm's productivity.

More than likely, he will want to see a demonstration and give me an appointment. He sees the product, likes it, and ABC Hosiery Company is no longer an unknown or even a prospect, but a customer.

More Ways the Telephone Can Increase Sales

The telephone system has no favorites. It works for anyone at any time, good, bad, or indifferent. The help a phone gives you in selling depends entirely on the use you make of it.

For example, suppose you have a five-day campaign planned for Philadelphia. Eight of the firms in your category give you appointments. Out of the eight, you sell five. By making the phone your junior salesman, you have averaged a sale each day. How long would that have taken you through letter writing or calling on those on the list "cold," door to door so to speak?

Through judicious use of the telephone, a salesperson makes the best use of his time and energy. It enables him to be very efficient.

Running around in circles takes energy and does not produce results. Many otherwise good salespersons, foundered on the rocks of discouragement, could be turned into real producers by making the telephone their junior salesman.

Another group of salespersons who cover large territories, possibly several states, spend way more money covering that in person than it would take to use the phone. Traveling several hundred miles only to find the prospect not available is a very great waste of time, money, and effort.

If a prospect will not make an appointment to see you over the phone, nine times out of ten he or she will not see you if you arrive in person. If you do get an interview under those circumstances, it will be only for courtesy's sake. Your chances of doing business with that person are very slim.

Making appointments by telephone teaches you to put a value on your time, trains you to be more specific and definite about your product, and perfects your voice and speech techniques. The prospect will react with more respect to a salesperson who approaches him or her in a more professional manner.

Therefore, it is obvious that making advance appointments by phone adds to the prestige and dignity of a salesperson. It shows that he or she is putting a value on his own time and is respecting the time of the prospect by not "butting in" inopportunely.

Appointment-Selling Increases Your Prestige

The salesperson who makes appointments in advance is much more likely to get the business than one who just "drops in."

In selling some products, an initial visit must be followed up by a demonstration before a committee or a group of people. To see each of them individually would consume enormous blocks of time and entail considerable expense. In this case, the telephone can be utilized very efficiently. Each person involved could be contacted by phone with a preliminary discussion, then a time arranged to suit everyone.

In this situation, the telephone should be combined with the mail approach. Send each individual a confirmation letter to follow up the phone conversation and to remind him or her of the appointment not long before the scheduled time.

Most physicians and even beauty salon operators will call the day before an appointment to remind the patient or customer. Professionals have learned how to save time and energy in other fields through use of the phone. Why not those in the sales field?

Some time ago, I was discussing the idea of telephone appointments with one of Oklahoma's top business executives. He gave me an interesting example of why this is so efficient and increases sales.

One of his salesmen was working on a deal that required him to see a number of people. One of these men lived in Austin, Texas, several hundred miles away. The executive suggested to the salesman that he call the prospect in Austin and make an advance appointment. However, the salesman refused, saying he would have a better chance by driving to Austin and just dropping in.

I am sure you can predict the end of this story already! When the salesman arrived in Austin, he found his prospect had been called out of town. Five hundred miles of travel, gallons of gasoline wasted, valuable hours of selling time lost, much personal energy burned up, and for what? The effort, money, and time involved were "gone with the wind."

One short, inexpensive phone call would have saved all that. The salesman did not use his head, nor did he accept a suggestion from the executive. I do not see that man going very far in any field simply because he is a personality who has to learn the hard way. Also, he showed lack of respect for someone in authority and could not recognize wisdom when he heard it.

Every Call Is Money in Your Pocket

Selling is not static, but dynamic. It is a process that involves keeping in motion. By using the telephone for sales or to make appointments, a salesperson can extend his or her personality, broaden influence, and capitalize on selling ability.

Keep a record of your calls and add them up every month or so. You will be surprised at the value of these calls to you simply in money earned and time saved.

By using the telephone and systematically going down a list in the phone book of firms or individuals in your sales field, you will hit many more prospects than by simply picking and choosing on whom to call.

If you do not pass up prospects but call each, combing the territory thoroughly, you will find customers you never dreamed existed. Here are a few hints in making successful calls:

Use a distinct, well-modulated, natural and unaffected tone. Your voice should convey personal interest and genuine earnestness in the service you are endeavoring to render.

Speak clearly into the mouthpiece, holding it not more than three-fourths of an inch from your lips. This enables the prospect to hear you distinctly. Just as there is no need to shout at a prospect in his or her office, there is no need to use a loud tone over the phone.

Breathe deeply before beginning and speak slowly enough to be understood the first time. Talking rapidly or slurring your words makes "What did you do?" sound like "Wadjado?"

Be positive in your remarks, speak with authority but not with an overbearing tone or attitude which conveys arrogance or presumptuousness.

Sound cheerful. No one wants to spend much time talking to someone who is "down in the dumps" or sounds as if he or she had just lost his best friend.

New ideas, expressed in new products can greatly expand the national income of the United States as well as a salesperson's individual income. Men and women who sell can further this expansion by using the telephone as a tool to reach more people.

What is behind the door, I do not know,
But this I know and know it well:
The more doors I open, the more I sell!

CHAPTER 21

A Letter the Prospect Will Remember

For those occasions when writing a letter is more appropriate or more convenient, the same guidelines apply as for telephone contacts. There are many books available on business letter writing.

The 19th century author Robert Louis Stevenson could wax lyrical about the "marvelous possibilities" contained in a blank, meaningless piece of white paper.

A blank piece of paper does hold great possibilities. Of course, man is not born into this world automatically able to write a good letter. However, letter writing is like swimming: the ability can be acquired. It is a skill, not a talent. If developed properly, it can be an art.

Any salesperson can learn to write an effective letter, although some time and effort must be devoted to the development of good technique. Most artists must learn the techniques of their particular field—oil painting, water colors, portraits, still lifes, and so forth—before becoming adept.

A letter is a record of your thoughts and reveals something about your personality, unless it is cold and formal. In that case, it will not attract the attention of the one who receives it and may end up in "File 13".

A letter on which you have spent some time and thought gives your prospect something to ponder.

Before setting out to arrange interviews through letters, it would be good to study letters written by most businesses in order to see what not to do! Most such letters are boring with "catch phrases," cliches, and/or the jargon of the writer's particular field.

Use them as a guide and write the opposite, then you will be on your way to learning how to write a good letter that attracts the attention of the one receiving it.

As a salesperson, you can acquire the art of writing a good letter. You can become adept at visualizing thoughts and ideas through the written word. There is no need to become tense and feel as if you are writing an Academy Award speech.

Relax, be yourself, try to be perfectly natural. Formality retards establishing the connection with the prospect. On the other hand, sloppy informality can be just as offputting. Try to feel as though the person to whom you are writing is sitting right across from you.

Shakespeare wrote that "brevity is the soul of wit" — a good thought! Therefore, do not be long-winded in a letter anymore than you would in person. That bores the prospect and pushes him or her away as if you literally pushed them from you.

Do not tell the prospect everything you know in a letter, but just enough to pique interest in you and your product.

A warm but brief letter is the best way I know, outside of a phone call, of creating a favorable impression and eliciting a favorable reply.

Learning how to write business letters well enough to impact the customer will enlarge your ability to sell and broaden your influence.

First impressions, whether by phone, by letter, or in person, are extremely important. Many times, if that first impression is unfavorable, you do not get a chance to correct it or to replace it with a more favorable one.

The tone or attitude is very important, but it is also necessary to know the right structure for a business letter in order to appear professional.

How a Good Letter Is Constructed

A letter can be divided into five parts: the salutation or greeting, the opening sentence (what newspaper people call "the lead"), the heart of the letter or the main body, the close (words that sum up the letter), and the signature.

I believe the salutation should always be personalized, not a generic greeting. In other words, "Dear Mr., Ms., or Mrs. Sloan," instead of "Dear Sir, Ms., or Madam." The generic greeting could apply to anyone.

The opening sentence should grab the reader's attention. Sometimes a question is a good beginning: "Have you ever thought . . . ?" In the life insurance business, it might be, "Have you ever considered what would happen to your business if you were not around?"

The heart of the letter then must expound on your opening statement or question. Organize in notes what you want to convey. Be direct and to the point. Do not ramble, beat around the bush, or be obscure. Nor should you try to be "cute". Use plain, concise, understandable language.

I suggest first organizing notes of what you want to say, then writing a sample letter. Incorporate every idea you have pertaining to the subject at hand even if you know it is too long and too wordy.

Let it "sit" for a while, then go back and reread it as if you were the recipient. Imagine getting that letter from a company with which you are not familiar, then:

Analyze and review the material.

Take out what is superfluous.

Arrange the points in the right sequence to lead the receiver's thoughts from one idea to another in order.

Replace any of the words with others that seem to suit the prospect's field better.

The close of any letter should be a brief summary of the main points. Use short, crisp sentences that carry an impact. Be certain that your tone is respectful.

As for the signature, always sign your name in a natural way after "Respectfully yours," or "Sincerely yours," or "With best regards," or something similar.

The main purpose of a sales letter is to be your advance agent that will open the door for you and tell the prospect something about you and your product before he sees you.

Now that you have the structure of a business letter in mind, let us talk about how to write such letters effectively.

How To Write Effective Business Letters

A letter, just as a person-to-person call, is a meeting of two minds. Therefore, the letter should convey the facts and circumstances in a manner that will influence, persuade, and convince. The ability to assemble a few platitudes or string a few sentences together will not achieve this objective.

Make it a habit to use your imagination to anticipate the effect your letter will have on the recipient. Ask yourself what purpose you hope to achieve and what is the best way to do this. The first part is easy: to gain an appointment with this prospect. The second part will require some thinking.

You want to have an easy flow of meaty, strong words with a punch. Your letter must be explicit, simple, and brief. Here are some examples of the hearts of letters that have worked for me:

> *Would you like to increase your output 33 1/3 percent? That is exactly what we did for a recent client who was having difficulty showing a reasonable profit on orders booked.*

> *How is your "profit picture"? Are your profits smaller due to rising costs of materials and labor or to inadequate control of production costs? Outside help for inside problems is one way progressive managements have been able to increase profits.*

> *We may be able to help you and would like an opportunity to outline our methods in person, by phone, or by follow-up correspondence. Of course, none of these communications involve any obligation to you.*

This letter said just enough to arouse interest, but not enough to sound "pushy" or to be boring.

How Letters Can Increase Sales

Letters can increase your sales. If your first attempt does not bring a response, try again along a somewhat stronger line. Here is a sample letter to a prospect who has not responded to previous attempts at contact.

> *For the past few months, you have "locked your door" against me. Obviously, it pays to lock your door against a thief, but I am not even a thief of time! In fact, I can prove that a few minutes loaned to me will return compound interest to you.*
>
> *If everyone locked their doors against one another, how quickly we would become another Iron Curtain Country. The exchange of ideas has made the United States great, and I know of no better way to keep it that way.*
>
> *I will stop by to see you on Thursday at 10 a.m. Believe me, I can see the key to your door in your hand, as I know you can see the value of exchanging ideas. Looking forward to seeing you and with high regards and best wishes for your continued good health and happiness, I am (conclude with signature).*

The following letter will always arouse curiosity in a prospect and usually provoke a response:

> *An important situation now confronts your company that can easily affect its entire future operation. I will visit your office Wednesday at 10:30 a.m. to give you the facts.*
>
> *I believe you will have no doubt that the time allotted for my appointment will be of great service to you.*

With high regards and good wishes for the continued success of your company, I am (signature).

The next letter does everything but provide an application:

Have you considered that it takes $100,000 invested in 6 percent bonds to result in an income of $500 a month?

To have this amount of income at retirement requires savings of almost $10,000 a year for the next 20 years. To save that amount per year after taxes, living expenses, and educational or additional expenses, is almost an impossibility.

However, Mr. Smith, you can achieve the same result for only $125 a week. In fact, you can do better than the savings plan above. This insurance plan also guarantees that if you should pass away while making these investments, my company will return all your payments and pay your family $50,000 in cash. The plan also has other valuable features.

This is the most talked of plan anywhere. If you would like to know more about it, just mail the enclosed, stamped postcard.

Another sample letter along this line is addressed to "Mr. Doe" or to his family:

If you will fill in your date of birth below, I will submit a plan for your consideration that will cover medical expenses and disability income. This is the most discussed policy in the insurance field today.

Then below the usual signature, write: Name, address, date of birth, and provide lines for the information to be filled in and returned.

All of the above letters are simply patterns to follow, not models to copy. Copying another person's letter verbatim ends up sounding stilted. Adapt the examples to your own personality and situation.

Remember that your letter is your representative.

Make it neat on clean, fresh stationery.

Copy over any blots, blobs of ink, or erasures.

Writing good letters will definitely increase sales.

Also, do not lose sight of the fact that everything does not succeed on the first try. How many modern inventions would we not have today if inventors had stopped trying before they succeeded? There always have been those who said, "It cannot be done." Experts can be wrong, and many like these have been.[1]

1840 — "Anyone traveling at the speed of 30 mph would surely suffocate."

1878 — "Electric lights are unworthy of serious attention."

1901 — "No possible combination can be united into a practical machine by which men shall fly."

1926 — "This foolish idea of shooting at the moon is basically impossible."

---

[1] Bland, Glenn. Success, (Wheaton, IL: Living Books, Tyndale House Publishers, Inc., 1972), p. 18.

CHAPTER 22

How To Make Imagination a Junior Salesman

In addition to making this book and the telephone "junior salesmen" in your business, there is a "tool" within yourself that can be turned into another "junior salesman." That is the function of imagination.

During the last half of the 15th century, a young boy living in Genoa, Italy, helped his father as a wool weaver. At school, he studied Latin, mathematics, and astronomy. However, in his spare time, he visited the busy harbor and watched the coming and going of ships from many ports unfamiliar to him.

He listened to the tales of the rugged seamen on the docks. He was fascinated and inspired by the stories of the far away places these men had visited. Soon his imagination led him into the study of ship navigation. He became very skilled at making maps and charts.

He pictured himself as a seafaring man embarking on new voyages, finding new routes to open up trade with exotic countries, making new discoveries, and perhaps finding new lands. That is exactly what Christopher Columbus did when he grew up.

People who pioneer new methods, make new improvements, find new routes, make new discoveries, and invent new things follow in the same use of imagination as Columbus. They dare to do things that others think cannot be done. While others falter or tread the same old paths, they go forward along uncharted ways.

Someone who makes sales his or her path in life can do the same. He or she does not need "pull" or so-called influential friends, only to make imagination a "junior salesman," that can become a gold mine.

What is imagination?

It is the ability to think in terms of images as well as words.

It is the work of the mind, the power to envision new ideas and plans in action, then to transform them into useful service.

It is looking at present conditions or circumstances with a view to improving them.

The trigger to start imagination working for you is to ask yourself "what if" in any situation.

What if a machine could be built to sew much faster, neater, and more efficiently than seamstresses can by hand? After hundreds of years, Elias Howe dared to imagine this, and in 1846 we got the sewing machine.

I want to make a few suggestions that will illustrate ways and means of putting your imagination into positive action.

Five Ways to Improve Your Imagination

Train your imagination to "think" in pictures.

Once you ask "what if," try to picture the end result of doing things differently than at present. As you develop this ability, ideas will begin to flow. Pictures will begin to form in your mind. Your outlook will be broadened and your wits sharpened.

In 1969, I sold a young businessman a $10,000 life insurance policy. He was engaged in a very favorable business with unusual possibilities for development. However, I could see that he was not fully aware of his possible potential.

It seemed to me he needed an infusion of ideas in order to stimulate his slumbering imagination. Of course, I did not tell him this. Instead, I began to feed him ideas of a constructive and creative nature about his business. It was like adding yeast to dough! I could almost see his imagination begin to rise.

He developed a new attitude and outlook, a new zest for life, and a new enthusiasm for his business which became an avenue for creativity, not just a means of making a living. Over the next ten years, my input into his thinking also paid off for me. I sold him a total of a million dollars worth of insurance, an average of an additional $100,000 a year.

The moral is use your imagination for the benefit of others, if you see possibilities in their lives or businesses. By helping them, you may help yourself.

Train Your Imagination By Thinking

Every improvement in selling is brought about by imagining something better.

Ask yourself, "How can my selling imagination be improved?"

Analyze every part of your sales plan and presentation.

Think about each sentence you use: Could it be said differently and better? Why are you using exactly those words?

This process will begin a train of thought that will soon develop into a new and better way to say and/or do things. Very few sales plans are perfect. Imagination is the key to seeing any improvements.

In July 1986, the economy and the life insurance business had slowed, and I undertook to sell myself out of the recession. Starting with that premise, I saw in my imagination how to bring others to my viewpoint. I had fifteen thousand cards printed with this sentence: "We absolutely refuse to become part of the Recession of 1986."

To make this idea pay off, I had to put business first in my life. My imagination went to work drafting a sales presentation with this premise as its foundation, one that could be used via my other "junior salesman," the telephone.

Five months later, my goal had been accomplished. My bank account showed a handsome new balance. That was the first year I became the number-one agent out of fourteen thousand agents working for the second largest life insurance company in the nation. This was the experience that sold me on the use of the telephone in sales.

I sold $10 million in life insurance over the telephone, as a result of using my imagination. In fact, I sometimes sold as much as $50,000 worth of insurance without ever seeing the prospect. After the sale was made, the prospect would come by my office (not me going to his or hers) and sign the completed application for my secretary.

How can you know what you can do for the prospect until you analyze and visualize all the aspects of his or her business. As you gather information for the benefit of one customer, it helps you to see what also will benefit another customer.

Many businesses have the same basic needs, so improvements or benefits for one can be transferred to another. Ask yourself these questions to stir your imagination:

Is there any way to improve this business?

Is the owner or manager fully aware of present opportunities?

Is anything lacking in present procedures?

Can I offer a suggestion or idea to improve this business?

How can I obtain additional sales from this business and still serve this prospect?

Have I only half-sold this prospect and left the field wide open for a competitor to come in behind me?

Ideas are very similar to the old saying about lightning. They may not strike but once in the same place. The time to act on an idea is when it hits you. If you get in the habit of quick action on ideas from your imagination, more ideas will follow.

Train Your Imagination By Observing Children

Children can teach us a very valuable lesson in the development of imagination. As we grow older, unfortunately our imaginations tend to atrophy for lack of use.

The late scientist Albert Einstein once told the mother of a neighborhood child who came to him for help with homework that he had learned more from the child than she had from him. A Chinese proverb says it is only the wise who appreciate that the truly great person keeps a childlike (not childish) view of life.

Jesus Himself told His disciples that to truly understand how to follow Him they must "become as little children" (Matt.

18:4,5). Taking my little granddaughter, Rebecca, out for a stroll helps me to open up my imagination. She sees four little ducks sitting on a log where I saw nothing. She sees a flock of pigeons while I am thinking of what to do tomorrow.

I thought, "And a little child will lead them (Isa. 11:6) into the kingdom of imagination as well as into other invisible kingdoms that are more real than our social, cultural, and professional kingdoms."

Children who have been reared in loving, safe homes are free from doubt, free from dread, free from distortion, and free from inhibitions. As we grow older, we develop "walls" of fear, doubt, self-consciousness, unforgiveness, and other negative emotions that cloud our imaginations.

Try to pull down all these things that inhibit your ability to think past tradition, past the "way things are always done," and past fear of what others will think.

Train Your Imagination To Ask Questions

Every question mark is a hook, and if you put out enough hooks, you are bound to "catch" some ideas. Often, ideas from your imagination will enable you to anticipate the needs of a prospect, in the process triggering his imagination.

Some years ago, I telephoned a manufacturer whom I had never seen concerning life insurance. His reaction was that he was not interested so I would be wasting my time calling on him. At that point, I moved away from the subject of life insurance and began to ask about his business.

This question started the flow of ideas. I found he was anxious to talk, telling me about a recent $125,000 addition that had been made to his plant building. He even told me what the mortgage amount was on the company. My imagination clicked into gear.

I pointed out that a life insurance policy on him would immediately pay off the mortgage in the event something happened to him. On the other hand, if he lived another ten years, the policy would have accumulated enough to pay off the mortgage anyway. Imagination made another sale for me and had been of great benefit to the prospect.

Prospects are not usually dumb, but open-minded. Sincere questions provoke ideas, arouse responses, stimulate interest, create a desire, and give you the inside track on how to accomplish your goal and that of the prospect.

Train Your Imagination To Gather Ideas

The best way to gather ideas is to pay strict attention to your environment. Many interesting things surround you most of the time. Imagination helps to classify them as to their importance.

We were given eyes with which to see, ears with which to hear, a mind with which to think, and an imagination with which to see not only what is but what could be. Apply these principles to your own affairs as well as to those of the prospect.

Imagination Is the Beginning of Creativity

The late playwright and author George Bernard Shaw thought imagination was, "The beginning of creation. You imagine what you desire; you will what you imagine; and at last, you create what you will."[1]

Others put it this way:[2]

> *My mind's eye. [William Shakespeare]*
>
> *Means to make images and to move them about inside one's head in new arrangements. [Jacob Bronowski]*
>
> *A good horse to carry you over the ground—not a flying carpet to free you from probability. [Robertson Davies]*
>
> *The wide-open eye which leads us always to see truth more vividly. [Christopher Fry]*

---

[1] Webster's New World Dictionary of Quotable Definitions, edited by Eugene E. Brussel, (Englewood Cliffs, N.J.: Prentice Hall, a Simon & Schuster Co., 1988, 1970), p. 278.

[2] Ibid, p. 277.

CHAPTER 23

"Getting the Breaks" Is Not Luck

Reading books with good ideas and suggestions for sales and dealing with people is a good foundational step to waking up your own imagination. Make a habit of keeping up with current events through news magazines such as Newsweek, Reader's Digest, Forbes, and trade publications for the field in which you sell.

If you do not have money in your budget to subscribe to these publications, your local library usually has up-to-date copies. You can zerox any articles you want to keep. A library card is a great aid to developing imagination.

One book that I have read once a year for more than three decades is How I Raised Myself From Failure to Success in Selling by a man named Frank Bettger. It may be out of print; however, go to Amazon.com online. Many second-hand booksellers also offer such titles.

Try not to scan or read too quickly. Reading is like eating. Fast devouring may fill your mind or stomach, but you will not get the full flavor. What you digest, not what you take in feeds your entire system; likewise with what you read.

Do you ask yourself at times, "Why do other people always get the breaks?"

"Getting the breaks" is not simply a matter of fate or luck.

It is being prepared to take the break when you are in the right place at the right time. Opportunities come to those who prepare for them. Instead of complaining that others are somehow favored, begin to equip yourself with an active imagination which will enable you to take advantage of "the breaks."

As you read at a measured pace, your mind will throw up questions. Do not ignore these. Stop and consider each question. I have spent as long as half an hour on one sentence. Reading in this manner increases understanding and gives you an insight into the thinking of others. The old saying, "Two heads are better than one," is quite true.

"Breaks" come to those who have the ideas and imagination to develop opportunities. Following are names of three famous businessmen who "got the breaks" through using their imaginations:

Asa Candler took an antiquated formula, had an idea of how it could be transformed into a drink to sell, and invented Coca Cola.

Henry Ford had an idea for cheap transportation that would be faster than horses, turned his imagination loose on the idea, and "got the breaks" in the automotive industry.

Thomas A. Edison looked at a tungsten coil, and through imagination, invented the light bulb.

Nearly every well-known inventor or founder of a corporation involving new products or new applications of known products did so through ideas filtered through imagination, not through "getting the breaks."

Many others could have invented or formed businesses to market these products, but they did not. Why? Either they never asked enough questions to get ideas, never used imagination to develop the ideas, or did not take the last step without which the first two are rendered impotent. That last step is putting ideas and imagination into action.

Pass on the things you visualize to your prospects or incorporate them into your own sales plan and life—or both!

Even those things which seem bad and perhaps even disasters can sometimes be turned for the good of yourself and others through imagination.

Imagination has a sidekick, another function of our minds that sometimes we call "hunches." Actually, hunches are intuition, whose immediate source is the subconscious. Information filed away, plus ideas developed through the imagination but not consciously thought about, suddenly pop into our minds full-blown.

How To Turn "Hunches" Into Customers

Intuition is knowledge from within, a quick perception without conscious attention or reason. Some believe intuition involves ideas from God brought through our human minds.

Intuition is different from instinct, which is defined as "an inborn tendency to behave in a way characteristic of a species"[1], in our case, human beings.

Instinct causes you to dodge a falling object, raise your fists if someone comes at you, and run across the street if a car heads your way.

Intuition is the "ability to perceive or know things without conscious reasoning."[2]

Whatever the source, ignore "hunches" to your own hurt. Simply because the idea seems to "come out of nowhere" and is not the result of a knowable process of thought does not mean it is invalid. Check out such sudden thoughts and prove whether it is of value or simply an "off-the-wall" idea of no value.

One afternoon, as I was relaxing in my office, such a hunch seemingly came out of a clear sky, an intuition that I should call on the president of a rather large company in my area. I had discussed an insurance policy with him a few months before.

Following intuition, I called him and within ten minutes had qualified him to buy $2,000 worth of insurance. My "hunch" had proven valid and paid off. All salespeople should train themselves to recognize these sudden impulses or thoughts as intuitive "hunches" and act on them.

Act on them sooner rather than later. Suppose I had postponed calling this man? More than likely I would have lost a sale. He might have called a competitor instead of me if my name had not come to his mind, which I could not count on. Inspiration from this source fades quickly, like a check written with disappearing ink. Cash in on it immediately.

As a matter of fact, I had completed all of the chapters in this book when the "hunch" came to me that readers would appreciate a few comments on intuition. After searching my local library, I could find no books on "hunches," so I decided to include this chapter.

In reviewing your own experience, can you remember times when intuitions paid off, or other times when you wished that you had followed that sudden "hunch" to do or say something?

Pursuing your hunches may help you build a sales record that will qualify you for advancement, as well as add to your income as you go along. On the other hand, do not get lazy and rely solely on intuition to "get you the breaks."

One salesman went to the president of his company asking why, after twenty-five years experience, he had been passed over for sales manager.

The president answered, "You have only had one year's experience repeated twenty-five times!"

Merely putting in hours does not make sales or win promotions. Learn to use your spare time to develop your personality, your sales plan, and your abilities. Success does not come from repeating the same year's experience over and over.

Real profitable experience adds what you have learned in one year to what you had before, sometimes deleting things that are not worth retaining. Knowledge, wisdom, and skill gained through a wise use of time results in experience that counts for something and is worth building on.

How To Make Your Spare Time Work for You

There are twenty-four hours in each day, one hundred sixty-eight hours in each week. If you work a normal forty-hour week, that leaves one hundred and twenty-eight hours in which to sleep, eat, entertain, spend time with family, and improve yourself. Using only 10 percent of this time outside work will give you at least twelve hours to spend improving yourself.

A few hours each week spent in studying, meditating, and analyzing your week's progress will enhance your prospects and improve your capacity to perform well. It is as important to utilize your spare time well as it is to organize your work week.

Make the most of those twelve hours by outlining a program and sticking to it. Spare time is your property. The use you make of it can determine your overall progress in life. If you take care to use the minutes well, the hours will take care of themselves, and the days will take care of you.

Here are six suggestions to help you make the best use of your spare time:

1. Spend an hour a day reading, reflecting, and reviewing.

2. Spend several minutes a day listing every thought and question you have concerning a certain subject.

3. Write a sample letter, not using "I, me, my, and mine."

4. Try to talk at least fifteen minutes a day without using personal nouns or pronouns.

5. Write a sample article or essay every day explaining, reporting, or defining something.

6. Take at least fifteen minutes a day to review experiences with customers and prospects. This will help you discover their interests and get ideas for your next visit.

I promise you that all the inventors, entrepreneurs, and successful people mentioned in this book, along with thousands of other men and women, have made use of their spare time to develop their ideas, their "hunches," their experience. They have made their imaginations "junior partners" in their work.

In preparing this book, I have used my "junior partner" first in order to see myself in your shoes. Many books on sales are dull and uninteresting, not full of ideas or inspiring to the imagination. As I wrote, I asked myself these questions many times:

- Is this interesting?
- Is it instructive?
- Is it inspiring?
- Is what I am saying getting across the right ideas?

My touchstone for the answers has been, if I were starting out in sales, would this material be what I would want to read? Every idea has had one objective: the interest of the reader.

Will each idea stimulate thinking, inspire imagination, increase understanding, and contribute to the growth of the reader?

I have put a lot of my spare time, thought and effort into trying to make the reader a better salesperson, also a better man or woman.

Reread this chapter several times in order to take the brakes off your imagination, which will begin to "bring the breaks" to you. Learn to see the ducks, not just the log, as my granddaughter does.

Applying the ideas discussed in this chapter will be like hiring a "junior salesman" to help you for life. Try it! Start today, for this day is all you know for sure that you have.

Use your imagination to get charged up to move ahead.

Edmund Burke, 18th century British statesman and orator, wrote this on imagination that leads to lasting ideas:

> *The great difference between the real and the pretender is that the one sees into the future, while the other regards only the present; the one lives by the day, and acts on expediency; the other acts on enduring principles and for immortality.*

---

[1] Webster's New World Dictionary, p. 701.
[2] Ibid, p. 709.
[3] Edwards, Tryon; editor. The New Dictionary of Thoughts, (Standard Book Company, 1960), p. 407.

CHAPTER 24

How To Get Charged Up to Move Ahead

An electrical engineer whom I know once told me an electric battery is a self-contained unit of energy, ready to work. In other words, it is a combination of parts that produces an electric current. To work properly all the parts must be kept in good condition. The slightest impairment of any part will disrupt the battery's function.

You might say a salesperson can be compared to an electric battery. He or she is a self-contained unit of energy, a complete entity made up of three main components, yet still an individual. Each person has physical qualities (the body), mental and emotional qualities (the soul), and spiritual attributes (the spirit man or woman whose body is the "earth suit").

Each of these functions, when in good health and maintained properly, mean the person is well-adjusted and operating properly. It is a simple process to recharge an electric battery, but recharging a person is much more complicated. Each of man's functions has many interrelated parts.

First, let's consider the body for if it is not in good working order, nothing works right. The Apostle Paul called our bodies "temples." (1 Cor. 3:16.) The poet Oliver Wendell Holmes called his body a "house." Toward the end of his life, he told someone his "house" was not in good shape; however, he (the person within) was doing fine.

How To Assure Physical Health

Barring accidents and hereditary conditions, there are things we can all do to keep in good physical health. The Bible says the "life is in the blood" (Lev. 17:14), and science has pretty much shown this is true.

Four elements go into keeping the blood healthy. They are oxygen, food (vitamins, minerals, etc.), water, and sunlight. So how we do make sure we have the right ratios of these four?

1. Breathe deeply often. The lungs supply this need, so by all means inhale slowly and exhale deeply enough to make sure the carbon dioxide has been eliminated.

To get the full effect of breathing, you should breathe twelve times a minute. Time yourself and see how fast you breathe. A fast breather is a shallow breather; a slow breather usually is a deep breather.

Deep breathing empties the lungs, purifies the blood, strengthens the diaphragm, and helps you relax.

2. Check your diet with medical guidelines and be sure that you are eating healthily. Also, be sure to chew your food thoroughly. However, chewing too intensely and gulping your food down are both very ill-mannered habits, in addition to causing indigestion and other problems.

One day as I was having a cup of coffee, a young man came into the restaurant and sat across from me. He was pale and emaciated. I guessed that he had some sort of digestive trouble. He ordered two large hamburgers and a milk shake, all of which he ate in a minute and forty-five seconds!

I could not resist asking if he had stomach problems and if he always ate that fast. He replied that, yes, he did, and he had never thought about how fast he ate. I suggested that for his health, happiness, comfort, and peace of mind, he try slowing down and thoroughly chewing his food. He would certainly enjoy his food more, I said.

He could have resented my "butting into his life." However, he did not and instead took my suggestion. You should see him today! He looks like a new man, which he is.

Chewing stimulates saliva and the consistent outpouring of enzymes that help turn starch into sugar. Chewing food well lessens the work of the internal organs that process the food into fuel and energy.

3. Drink plenty of water. Three-fourths of the earth is water and so is 90 percent of your body. It does not take long to become dehydrated. Coffee, tea, juices, and soft drinks contain water, but not enough to keep the body in good health.

Water keeps the skin pores open and helps rid the body of toxins and waste materials. Dry climates and a lot of sun also deplete the body of moisture. You can live a number of days without food, but only about three without water. Doctors say the average person needs eight full glasses of water a day.

4. Walk in the sunshine. Even with all of the admonitions today about too much sun and skin cancer, doctors will tell you that some sunlight is necessary for your well-being.

Long sleeves, sunscreen for the harmful ultraviolet rays, sunglasses to protect your eyes, and a hat or cap for the top of your head will give you all the protection you need. In addition, walking a mile at least three times a week helps your heart.

How To Assure Mental Health

We might call this section, "Walk on the Sunny Side of the Street." To do that, you must think positively.

Positive thoughts are electricity on the job.

Positive thoughts are creative; negative thoughts are destructive.

Positive thoughts are light while negative thoughts are darkness.

Positive thoughts are based on confidence and faith; negative thoughts are based on ignorance and doubt.

Positive thoughts will burn holes in problems, as a match will burn holes in paper.

Positive thoughts have almost become cliches in the past twenty years. However, that does not mean they do not work to keep you in good mental health.

Try thinking positively one day and see how your day goes. Then the next day think negatively about yourself, everyone around you, and everything you do. Compare the difference in results for yourself.

Here are five things that have helped me immensely in keeping a balanced state of mind:

1. Change your attitude from negative to positive and you will change your conditions. A good attitude is developing the right slant on what you are doing. You cannot sell successfully (or do anything else for that matter) if you are not positive about it. Enthusiasm for your work or your product cannot be faked but begins in the mind.

2. Align your thoughts and ideas. You cannot get good, helpful ideas to carry you onward if your thoughts about what you do are negative, any more than your vehicle will run smoothly with one tire pointed one way and another the opposite way.

3. Question your state of mind if you find yourself getting discouraged or depressed. Either your thoughts have gone negative or your ideas have dried up for lack of imagination, lack of interest, or a subtle attack of negativity.

4. Do not become a slave to anything. Addictions are not always confined to the body. A person can become addicted to feeling sorry for himself or to "wallowing in the blues" or to self-pity.

Endeavor to get a true picture of yourself and do not let anyone, anything, or any circumstances convince you that you are not capable, worthwhile, and potentially successful.

5. Periodically take stock of where you are, where you have been, and where you are going.

How To Assure Spiritual Health

The greatest of all power is treated in most areas of life with only a passing glance. As a salesperson, learning to appropriate spiritual power in one's work will be invaluable. No one can discover or appropriate spiritual power for you. You must do it for yourself.

There are only two sources of spiritual power: God, the Creator, and man's greatest enemy, the fallen angel called Lucifer. However, part of God's provision to those who believe on Him through His Son, Jesus the Christ, is the Holy Spirit.

Those who have not been "born again" as new creatures (2 Cor. 5:27) are lacking access to the greatest Counselor (Isa. 9:6) in the universe.

The pressure of life and the pace of everyday activities tempts us to think we do not have time or opportunity for meditating on the Word of God and praying.

You have to consider this as part of your "Research Department." Most large concerns have greatly increased the quality and quantity of their products because of their research department. The skilled researchers spend their days looking for new products, testing the ones already being made, and ways to improve existing products.

The time you spend "researching" the spiritual power available to you from the Divine Source will add immeasurably to your sales ability as well as your personal life.

From my years of experience in selling, I know that spiritual power works, as it is the Holy Spirit coming alongside a child of God to help. Of course, to get this help, you must be living out God's plan for your life and walking in His way. Too many of those who belong to God keep Him and His power separated from their everyday lives.

They expect that power to manifest in church on Sunday and when they panic and call on God in emergencies or times of crises. However, too many do not learn to treat God as a partner, or "co-pilot" as the old World War II song said. So in their everyday lives, spiritual power is absent because they shut out the Source of it.

"I'll do it my way" has become society's theme, the slogan, and the principle to live by in the past half century. Man's way throughout history has ended in downfall and disaster in every nation and society. Only God's way — and every religion is not following God's way — ends in success.

Many great men of the past have made this realization a reality in their lives not as an abstract theory. They drew on advice from the Holy Spirit, appropriated divine ideas and principles, and applied them to their activities. The result was creativity, personal success, and benefit for society.

<u>Definitions To Live By</u>

The best day .... today.
The greatest handicap .... fear.
The easiest thing to do .... find fault.
The most useless characteristic ..... pride.
The greatest mistake .... giving up.
The greatest satisfaction .... work well done.
The most disagreeable person .... a complainer.
The cause of mental bankruptcy ... loss of enthusiasm.
The greatest necessity .... common sense.
The best medicine .... forgiveness.
The greatest thing in the world ..... love.
The greatest friend and helper ...... God.

CHAPTER 25

How To Take Off the Brakes

Do you feel as if you are driving through life with the brakes on?

Does it seem as if you are moving in slow motion, never quite reaching your goal?

I have found that the "brakes" usually are in your mind, the negative ideas and thoughts that we have talked about in previous chapters. King Solomon, known as the wisest man on earth in his lifetime, wrote: For as he thinketh in his heart, so is he (Prov. 23:7).

According to one of my good friends, a noted health director and head of the YMCA Health Club in Tulsa, every man has a busy day. He says this is what you did yesterday:

Your heart beat 103,689 times.
Your blood traveled 168,000 miles.
You breathed 23,040 times, inhaling 438 cubic feet of air.
You took in 3 1/4 lbs. of food and 2 9/10 lbs. of liquid.
You generated 4 tons of energy.
You exercised leg and arm muscles more than 1,000 times.
You moved 7 major muscles.
You exercised 7 million brain cells and spoke 4,800 words.

No wonder we are tired at the end of a day, even with little activity. All of that still means you can go through each day with the brakes on, so to speak. One example of getting up "raring to go," then forgetting to take off the emergency brake is a person who is temperamental or full of negative expectations of rejection.

A salesman who gets a rebuff first thing in the morning, then pouts or indulges in self-pity the rest of the day has pulled up his emergency brake. All of us, even those who overcome rebuffs with positive thoughts or take them in stride can learn a lesson from a good athlete.

An athlete who is successful warms up gradually. He takes his moves calmly and easily until he is thoroughly warmed up. On your calling list there always are a few who are easy to approach. If you begin the day by calling on these, you will be "warmed up" to tackle the tough ones.

A good beginning bolsters courage and buoys strength, and strength is in proportion to courage. Then you can work in a state of relaxation and freedom.

Also, as I wrote in the previous chapter, personal efficiency and mental alertness in selling are dependent on physical fitness. Physical fitness is not simply a matter of staying in good health but is determined also by your ability to relax.

A physically fit, relaxed, and calm salesperson will get things done, make the right decisions, exercise good judgment, and move into a rhythm of work that gets the day's work done with seemingly no effort.

If you learn to approach your days like this, you will find that by evening you are well-pleased with your efforts. You have created order in your life, and order is the first law of Heaven.

Relax, and watch your sales climb!

Relax, and your personality will be showcased. Negative thinking causes a rigidity of manner or creates a mask of phoniness that covers up your natural, likeable personality. Everyone has a measure of charm, that intangible quality that reaches out to and pleases others.

Charm may be compared to the pearl in the oyster. You do not know it is there until you "crack the shell." Charm brings out the best qualities within you that enrich your personality.

Six Rules To Enhance Your Charm

Can you improve your charm? Yes, just as every other quality or attribute, positive or negative, charm can be diminished, enhanced, or developed. I have found six rules or principles that will bring out or enhance your charm.

They are: adaptation, preparation, interest, praise, tolerance, and natural tendencies.

Adaptation

Simple biology shows us that all life adapts itself to its environment. A river does not argue or resent a rock, a hill, or a mountain. It cannot wear its way through the obstacle, it simply goes around it.

So learn to adapt yourself to the prospect's environment. Remember, your goal is to "get around" his obstacles, not to change or reform the prospect.

Preparation

You do not prepare for charm by having your face lifted, your nose straightened, your forehead widened, or by inserting a diamond in your front tooth, a tattoo on your arm, or a ring in your lip.

You must prepare on the firm foundation of being yourself. Pretense or "put-on" is swift and certain death to charm. A smile may win attention, but it takes charm to obtain results.

Interest

Where money is concerned, we give interest to get dollars or dollars to get interest. The same principle applies to people. To get dollars from the prospect, you must put forth interest. You must show interest by listening, by paying close attention to what the prospect says in order to truly hear, not just the words but the intention behind the words.

One of the finest shoe-shine operators in the world has his stand in the Tulsa Airport. I think nothing of going out of my way to have my good friend shine my shoes. In addition to his abilities in shining shoes, he is the essence of charm. He is always humble, gentle and polite. He is well-informed and listens intently to every word you tell him.

183

His gracious manner and friendly attitude telegraphs that he genuinely likes people. He makes you feel his day would not have been complete without your stopping by.

His business and life philosophy is, "You gotta treat people right."

Interest in others, kindness and humility of demeanor are always a part of charm.

Praise

Someone has said, "Praise is like a diamond. It derives its worth from its scarcity."

Praise is one of the greatest motivating forces to attract a prospect. It seems to be a law of nature that you increase whatever you praise. A sincere "pat on the back" fosters good will for you and contributes to the success and happiness of others.

If you want more sales, begin to praise the work you are doing. Praise magnifies good qualities and minimizes any bad ones. It is a positive expression of appreciation that expresses that you are pleased with the accomplishments of your prospect.

Praise gives approval to your prospect and his activities and lets him or her know you are interested in his welfare. It breaks down barriers and lets you in on situations that otherwise might be closed to you.

Praise might be termed "the Great Liberator." Therefore, when anyone deserves or earns your approbation, by all means give it. That will result in great dividends in your own life.

However, praise cannot be contrived or based on pretense. Look for something you can genuinely appreciate and praise. Do not fake praise; that will backfire and cost you dividends.

Tolerance

Everyone is entitled to his opinion in this country. Tolerance is respecting his opinion without necessarily agreeing with it or sharing in it. Tolerance gets rid of prejudice and hatred, and establishes a relationship on an even keel. It also aids in eliminating vanity.

Remember that the world was here when you came and will be here when you are gone. None of us singlehandedly can change the whole world. All we can do is change the "world" around us for the better. We do that many times by not trying to change things.

If the prospect is uncivil, give it no thought. Do not take it personally. He may be in a bad mood or having great problems about which you do not know. After all, his rebuff is not what is giving you the trouble: it is all the worry and negative thinking with which you are investing it.

Maintain a sense of humor. That leads to tolerance, peace of mind, and efficiency.

Natural tendencies

The first thing is to analyze your natural tendencies objectively and see what needs curbing and what needs training. A hippopotamus is very natural, but it is not as charming as a trained seal. The seal also is natural but has been trained so that his attributes which are endearing have been acquired through training.

If good habits and attitudes have been formed through training, they add to charm. Some people think charm is artificial. However, every improvement is "artificial" in a sense until it becomes part of you.

Charm is the art of pleasing others and, in the field of selling, is most essential. It increases poise, cleans and polishes the window of your personality.

Charm is a potent factor of effectiveness and makes it possible for you to present yourself at all times in the most favorable light.

Charm, to be real, is based on the number-one principle of getting along in life: Love your neighbor as yourself (Mark 12:31), which has become known as "the Golden Rule."

Two qualities always cause a salesperson to stand out of the crowd: trustworthiness and a respect for the prospect. It pays to conduct your relationships on a purely ethical basis. Make the Golden Rule your basic operating principle. Make yourself dependable and also indispensable.

Of course, that admonition is the second part of the commandment that sums up all the others. The first part is to love God with your whole heart. If you do that, loving your neighbor comes easy.

The Number One Rule of Success

The economic growth and strength of America is fundamental, dominating and perpetual. Our economy will continue to provide more of the good things of life to more people as more salespersons continue to plant ideas, influence people, and inspire them to live a better life.

As such a salesperson, you are a motivating force and a contributing factor in making a better nation and a more secure people.

You may be wondering what love has to do with selling.

Love, or compassion, or caring for others has many components that contribute to the success of any salesperson, any individual, and a nation at large.

Love is kindness, a feeling of respect and appreciation for the prospect that inspires you to contribute to his happiness.

Love is humility that keeps you from becoming "puffed up" over a little success.

Love is the generosity that frees you from envy and helps you rejoice in the success and well-being of others.

Love is the basis of true charm.

Love is the patience that endows you with the calm assurance that "all's well that ends well."

Love is the courtesy that allows you to be polite and even-tempered in the worst circumstances as well as the best.

Love is sincerity, truth-seeking, and the ability to see all sides of a proposition; i.e. love underwrites tolerance.

Love, applied to sales creates a genuine attitude of respect, consideration, and kindness.

Love eliminates self-importance, arrogance, and impudence, permeates every occasion with a spirit of good will and cooperation.

Love annihilates doubt, uncertainty, anxiety, worry, and dread, confusion and conflict. It removes stubbornness, tension, and all negative thinking.

After more than four decades of experience in every aspect of selling, I have discovered that love has more power and influence on my mental, physical and spiritual activities than any other quality or attribute I could have.

When I practice kindness and consideration for others, I seem to tap into a great reservoir of power and strength that enables me to perform at a much higher level of ease and efficiency.

My own personal statement of ethics and reflection of the Golden Rule, developed over those decades of experience is this:

> *With God's help in each situation, I will always endeavor to treat others the way I would want and expect them to treat me in the same situation.*

> *With God's assistance, I will be committed always to giving beyond what people and the law requires of me while carrying out any act of service in which my business and I are involved.*

In preparing this book, my sole purpose has been to inspire those who sell to equip themselves in order to be the best persons they can possibly be. I have endeavored to put forth ideas and thoughts that will increase not only selling ability but to make better, more "whole" and happy salespersons.

Each chapter has been developed around one thought: to give the reader practical ideas and suggestions concerning a salesperson's relations with prospects. In addition, these suggestions, if put into effect, will improve a person's relationships in any area.

My best wishes, hopes, and prayers go to everyone who reads this book. I have found no better prayer for a salesperson than that of the late Cardinal Richard Cushing:[1]

> *Dear God,*
> *Help me be a good sport in this game of life. I don't ask for an easy place in the lineup, just put me where you need me. I'll only ask that I can give you 100 percent of all that I have.*

> *If the hard drives seem to come my way, I thank you for the compliment. Help me remember that you never send in a player and have him do more than he can handle.*

Help me, Oh Lord, to accept the bad breaks as part of the game; and, may I always play the game on the square no matter what others may do.

Help me study the books so that I can know the rules. Finally, God, if the natural turn of events goes against me and I am benched for sickness or old age, please help me to accept that as part of the game too. Keep me from whimpering or squealing that I was framed or that I ruined a deal.

And when I finish the final inning, I ask for no laurels. All I want is to believe that in my heart I played as well as I could.

Amen.

---

[1] Prayer given by Cardinal Cushing many years ago at a Los Angeles Angels game.